Incentivology

Jason Murphy is an economist who has worked at the Australian Treasury, the Ministry of Finance of the Republic of Nauru, and the *Australian Financial Review*. He writes regularly for Crikey and News.com.au, blogs at thomasthethinkengine.com and has a passion for bringing economics into the everyday world.

Incentivology

The forces that explain tremendous success and spectacular failure

JASON MURPHY

Hardie Grant

BOOKS

Published in 2019 by Hardie Grant Books,
an imprint of Hardie Grant Publishing

Hardie Grant Books (Melbourne)
Building 1, 658 Church Street
Richmond, Victoria 3121

Hardie Grant Books (London)
5th & 6th Floors
52–54 Southwark Street
London SE1 1UN

hardiegrantbooks.com

 A catalogue record for this
book is available from the
NATIONAL LIBRARY National Library of Australia
OF AUSTRALIA

Incentivology
ISBN 978 1 74379 499 9

10 9 8 7 6 5 4 3 2 1

Cover design by John Canty
Cover image: ajt/Shutterstock.com
Typeset in 12/17 pt Adobe Garamond Pro Regular by Post Pre-press Group, Brisbane
Printed by McPherson's Printing Group, Maryborough, Victoria

 The paper this book is printed on is certified against the Forest Stewardship
Council® Standards. FSC® promotes environmentally responsible, socially
beneficial and economically viable management of the world's forests.

To Mum and Dad. Thank you.

Contents

Prologue ix

Introduction 1

Part 1: Incentives in Theory 9

    Chapter 1: The Power of Incentives 11

    Chapter 2: A Perverse Inclination 23

    Chapter 3: Unintentional 31

    Chapter 4: Missing Incentives 41

    Chapter 5: Your Brain on Incentives 51

    Interlude: A Mannish Jape 67

Part 2: Incentives in Action 73

    Chapter 6: Less Than a Loaf of Bread 75

    Chapter 7: Crazy Bargains (and Crazy Luxury) 93

    Chapter 8: Only the Fittest Survive 109

    Interlude: Dog 125

    Chapter 9: Self-perpetuating Incentives 135

    Chapter 10: Corruption and Rot 147

Chapter 11: Justice   169
Chapter 12: Injustice, Armour and Fire   185

Interlude: The Hunger Games   205

Chapter 13: Climate Change   211
Chapter 14: Ostrom   233

Conclusion: That Ball is Still in the Air   247
Acknowledgements   251
Endnotes   253

Prologue

Let me take you back in time.

It's the 1980s. I'm a small boy standing on an expanse of grass. From the sky, suddenly, arrives a projectile. It misses me narrowly and I'm stunned.

My father is trying to teach me to catch. I am basically enjoying the process. But it's straining against the limits imposed by a short lifetime spent mostly inside, mostly reading books.

I am uncoordinated and, worse, frightened of the ball. I catch a precious few, but too often I flinch. The ball bounces off my hands, off my arms, off my torso, spilling onto the grass of the public park near my family home.

The park seems, to a small boy, tremendously large. It has a cricket oval at one end and a grassy area at the other. There is a playground and a pathway and a cliff of exposed rock. (I later learn the park was once a quarry.) An old brickworks adjacent to the park has just been knocked down, and the dust being raised there now is from the construction of luxury housing.

I scurry to pick up the ball and throw it back towards my father. He collects the ball from where it lands and lobs it gently back to me. I do my best, pick up the ball, and throw it back.

Then I see my father tense his body. He bends his spine back so his face looks up into the blue sky, and draws his arm back. His arm springs upward and the ball is launched. It rises, higher and higher, until it appears tiny. I stand still on the grass, mouth agape, when I hear my father's voice.

'I'll give you a dollar if you catch it!'

—

We will leave this scene here, with the ball paused at the top of its parabolic arc, father and son frozen in a sunny tableau fraught with tension and expectation. My athletic self-esteem hangs in the balance like Schrödinger's cat, both alive and dead. I promise to resolve the story a little later.

But first, let's make sure we're on the same page about incentives.

Introduction

Reward and punishment are very different. They're like two mismatched characters thrown together in an action adventure movie. The duo don't get along but must go on a quest together. It is only over time that they discover what they have in common: an amazing power to make things happen.

We are about to meet this pair. Reward is first. We shall observe it in its natural habitat.

In 2016 an organisation called The Nature Conservancy put up a US$150,000 prize to anyone who could help them solve a major environmental problem: protecting marine life. Fishing boats in the Pacific Ocean haul from the briny deep all manner of species. Certain species of tuna in particular are overfished in contravention of the law, and the numbers being caught must be monitored. But how can we be certain what kinds of aquatic life are landing on deck?

Some Pacific fishing boats are fitted with cameras that record what is caught. Ingenious! But who will watch the videos? Paying marine experts to watch hour upon hour of flopping fish is one option, but the cost adds up. For every hour of fishing video collected, an expert must spend over 30 minutes classifying the catch. There are thousands of fishing vessels in the Pacific and they fish for weeks at a time.

This creates a viewing marathon that would outstrip even the most epic binge of *Deadliest Catch*, and with a lot less drama than that show. Using software to classify the fish being caught – the same sort of software used in facial recognition – could be a giant leap forward.

So could a machine-learning algorithm save time, save money and save marine life? The Nature Conservancy asked artificial intelligence experts to help find out.

The fisheries competition was run through a company called Kaggle. Kaggle uses prizes to motivate teams of people to solve problems in machine learning. (It was set up in 2010 by a young Australian entrepreneur called Anthony Goldbloom who, by chance, worked at the Australian Treasury at the same time as me.)

The power of the prize is enormous. The Nature Conservancy was able to attract a large volume of entries – 2293, to be precise – and among them was some top talent. The competition was won by a team of three machine-learning professionals with expertise in object classification who entered a sophisticated 'deep neural net' solution. Their algorithm not only classified fish caught during the day, but also those visible only on night vision cameras.

Cash rewards are a major part of the appeal of Kaggle. The fishing prize is not the biggest bait they've ever used. In 2017 a million-dollar Kaggle prize was offered to coders battling it out to create a better algorithm for estimating house values. A major real estate listing website called Zillow was the sponsor, and Zillow placed enormous faith in the answer the Kaggle competition provided. It began offering to buy certain houses, on the belief that this algorithm could tell the true value of a house. It was willing to put up the money to get the best result because it knew there would be long-term returns on that investment. And people were willing to put unpaid time into creating the best entry because of the potential cash reward.

But money is not the only appeal of Kaggle. The site provides gold, silver and bronze medals to entrants who may have missed cash prizes and hosts leaderboards that rank entrant performance across multiple competitions. Recognition accrues to the top-ranked individuals and teams. Social reward is a subtle but powerful part of the motivation – and this is true in general, not just at Kaggle.

Incentives of course include formal honours and awards: titles, prizes, badges, stripes on your shoulder. But informal status markers count too – how many people attend your parties, for example, and the contemporary equivalents: Twitter followers, Instagram likes, article clicks. Any system that can increase levels of social cachet can be used as an incentive, which is why social media has become an enormous incentive engine spitting out bizarre new rewards.

This book's second lead is an altogether uglier character. If reward is the good cop, punishment is the bad cop. Punishment brings the pain.

Fines. Prison. Being yelled at. Being publicly shamed. Punishments work differently from rewards. If you set up an incentive system that includes a punishment, you hope never to apply the punishment itself. The threat alone is supposed to deter the activity.

A perfect example of punishment in action is in the famous *Reinheitsgebot* – the German Beer Purity Law. Enacted in 1516 by Duke Wilhelm IV of Bavaria, the law stipulates the only permitted ingredients of beer: water, barley and hops (with yeast later added to the list). The reason that the law was enacted in the first place is disputed. Was it really about the purity of the beer, or was it about preserving wheat for use by bakers? History is murky, and the Reinheitsgebot has been the subject of numerous legal challenges, but it still exists to the current day.

What made the law stick? Why did brewers obey? The answer is punishment. The earliest versions of the Reinheitsgebot made deviations from the official recipe punishable by confiscation of the beer barrels, which would be done, according to the law, 'without mercy'. The prospect of losing their product and therefore their source of income made brewers take notice.

The Reinheitsgebot is seen as the first example of a food safety law. A similar concept applies in current Australian food safety laws, where restaurants can be shut down if they fail to comply. In some states, offenders are also named and shamed, with their misdeeds published online for 12 months. The threat of punishment is enough to ensure contemporary food safety standards are very high (at least as far as short-term infectious disease goes – long-term 'lifestyle' diseases are another matter …).

Kaggle has helped keep fish in the sea. Food safety laws have kept our beer pure – and probably saved countless lives as well. These are triumphs. And they have been achieved by careful application of incentives.

Meanwhile, careless application of incentives has created substantial disasters. This is most notable in the financial sector. Egregious examples that have come to light in Australia involve salespeople selling insurance that will never pay out, and making dangerously large loans by mis-classifying people's incomes and expenses. Employees were rewarded for doing so and faced no punishments. In America, similar incentives not only created loans that could not be paid back, but precipitated a collapse in the entire financial system that we call the Global Financial Crisis.

In all these scenarios – good and bad alike – people acted in the way particular incentives suggested to get the reward or avoid the punishment. Despite some negative outcomes, the message can be an extremely optimistic one: incentives make things happen. That is terrific news for anyone dissatisfied with the current state of the world. If we pay attention to incentives, we can control how they affect people in order to make change.

—

British philosopher Jeremy Bentham wrote that 'Nature has placed mankind under the governance of two sovereign masters, pain and pleasure.'[1] Bentham made this observation in the eighteenth century – long before neuroscientists peered into the brain and figured out why it was true.

Pain and pleasure come from systems in the human brain that drive us toward reward and away from punishment. Our brains throb with impulses that help us make life-sustaining choices – such as eating nourishing food and not placing our hand in a flame. Incentives exploit those natural systems. 'Artificial' rewards or punishments may be purposely designed or they may arise accidentally, but they drive our behaviour naturally by creating sparks of pleasure and pain where they would otherwise not have existed.

Incentives require more than just the prize or the punishment. This book often uses the term 'incentive system'. An incentive system includes the rules that define when an incentive is delivered and the people that keep watch to see if the rules are obeyed. Incentive systems are not always simple – they may include more than one kind of reward, or a mix of rewards and punishments. Incentive systems might be created by a government, a company, or, as we shall see, by complete chance.

Competitions and laws are obvious kinds of incentives. But incentives – particularly the accidental ones – can be camouflaged. They can change our actions without us ever being truly aware of them.

That hidden factors can affect human behaviour has recently returned to prominence in the idea of 'nudges'. Nudges are small, surprising psychological interventions that change behaviour: things like painting zigzag lines on a road to make people slow down, or encouraging taxpayers to pay tax on time by telling them 90 per cent of people pay on time. Nudges are not the same as incentives. They are just little tweaks to the way the world appears.

Nudge practitioners love to talk about 'choice architecture' – the way in which decisions are presented. For example, if you make people organ donors by default and give the choice to opt out, you end up with far more organ donors than if you presume people are not willing to be donors and give them the choice to opt in. The choices are ultimately the same – be an organ donor or don't. There is no explicit pressure. But the nudge implies donation is the social norm, and also relies on our tendency to minimise effort. That is enough to change behaviours. It turns out our behaviours are far more contingent on external factors than we realise.

Nudges have been particularly embraced by governments. Nudge experts are like archaeologists, digging into the real world to uncover micro-level motivations that have previously been ignored. And they have found that a lot of behavioural phenomena are not fixed. People's actions – driving too fast, not paying tax on time, not registering as organ donors – are influenced by these tiny hidden features.

The same is true of incentives – but on a larger scale.

Incentives can be hard to recognise, but they are rarely tiny. Once we realise the way they work, we will see plenty lurking in plain sight. Of course, many of the most astounding incentive problems come from classic issues – like contracts that give the other party far too much wriggle room. But some fascinating insights come from recognising that incentives are far more widespread than we ever dared realise.

—

Each of us has changes we would like to make, things we would like to achieve. It might be losing a few kilograms. Solving a problem at work. Ending global warming – you know, the usual stuff. With the application of the right incentives, behaviour patterns that looked stuck suddenly loosen. Of course, finding the right incentives is not easy. Mustering the power to apply these incentives is not trivial. Making sure the incentives don't get gamed is an endless Sisyphean task that might frustrate you for eternity. But incentives can make things happen on all scales – on ourselves, at home, at work or in the world at large. And seeing the many spectacular ways in which incentives go wrong helps us learn from the mistakes of others.

The next quote comes not from a famous philosopher, but from a blogger and software engineer called Jai Dhyani. He says this: 'Almost no one is evil. Almost everything is broken.'[2]

The more I learn about incentives, the truer that seems. The pages of this book catalogue human behaviour spiralling into the realm of the unexpected. Each time it would be possible to scapegoat the people that acted that way. And each time incentives were behind it.

I've often noticed that the naive and the powerful have something in common – the disregard of the limits that bind everyone else. The difference is in understanding how the world works. I believe we should 'think naive and act cynical'. Thinking naive means never giving up the idea we can make the world work differently. Acting cynical means knowing you can't achieve those naive goals by hoping everyone will see the light. Actions depend on incentives. The more skill we have in understanding rewards and punishments, the greater the power we gain to turn those 'naive' thoughts into reality.

Part 1

Incentives in Theory

Chapter 1

The Power of Incentives

Galileo couldn't figure it out. The great Italian astronomer had worked his whole life on a way to help ships' captains determine precisely where they were as they bobbed on the featureless sea. But this was a problem even he could not fully resolve.

The problem in question was longitude. In the seventeenth and eighteenth centuries ships could determine their latitude (their distance from the equator): they would simply check the sun's position at noon. But longitude was a mystery. The best available method was estimating your speed and plotting your position on a map. Relying on this approach meant land had a horrifying tendency to loom out of the dark unexpectedly. Shipwrecks were common.

Galileo's best attempt was a device that will shock nobody familiar with his work – it was a sort of telescope. He called it a celatone, and its lenses were affixed to a helmet. Once it was strapped in place on your head, all that remained was to observe the moons of Jupiter in their orbits.

History does not record if Galileo ever set foot on a ship. But seafaring types quickly figured out that standing on deck in a pitching sea and training your helmet-mounted eyepiece on the moons of Jupiter was insufficiently practical. While the celatone worked in theory, a more workaday solution was needed.

In 1714 the British Government promulgated the *Longitude Act* to try to solve the problem. The *Longitude Act* was pretty simple: it offered cash prizes to whoever could come up with a way to figure out longitude. If you could determine longitude within one degree and prove it on a transatlantic trip, you'd be eligible for £10,000 (equivalent to almost A$3 million today). If you could pin down the ship's longitudinal position even more tightly, you could pocket twice that. It sparked a frenzy of competition as England's intellectual elite vied for the reward.

The top prize would eventually be awarded to a man by the name of John Harrison. Harrison was 21 when the prize was announced and 37 when he tested his first prototype (it failed miserably on a trip to Lisbon). Many more prototypes followed before finally, at age 68, he sent his first successful device to sea. Disputes arose about whether its accuracy could be trusted or if it was a matter of luck, and Harrison was given only part of the prize.

Harrison's work relied on using accurate time-keeping to determine longitude. The challenge was coming up with a mechanical timepiece that would keep time on an ocean voyage. Thanks to the prize, Harrison – a carpenter and clockmaker by trade – devoted his life to overcoming that challenge. His device was called a marine chronometer.

Captain James Cook took a marine chronometer on his voyages through the South Pacific and raved about it. By the nineteenth century no ship left England without one. And while shipwrecks continued, they were far fewer and only very rarely due to the sudden and surprise appearance of entire continents. Harrison was awarded the rest of the longitude prize – only after appealing directly to the king – at age 80.

Prizes are powerful. Even though the payoff may be uncertain and potentially far in the future, the incentive effect reaches through time to overcome doubt and make things happen. Attaching a prize to an outcome can make that outcome a reality far sooner than it would otherwise have been. The lessons of the *Longitude Act* are certainly no secret, and the prizes offered since have birthed technological innovations with a proud history of dramatically transforming the world.

On a May evening in 1927, a man arrived in Paris. Men had been arriving in Paris for centuries, of course – but none before had come like this: by air, direct from the United States of America.

The man was 25-year-old aviator Charles Lindbergh. He had endured a solo 30-hour flight from New York, through fog and terrible weather. Lindbergh's tiny aircraft touched down in Paris – fuel tanks all but empty – just after 10 pm. He stepped onto French soil to a roaring reception.

Among the people who rushed to greet him was Raymond Orteig, a wealthy hotelier. He had posted a prize of US$25,000 for the first New York to Paris flight seven years earlier. Over those seven years planes flew further and further, and by 1926 aviators came to believe a flight of such endurance might be possible. In 1927, Lindbergh took off into appalling conditions and stayed aloft long enough to make the dream into a reality. As Lindbergh pocketed the $25,000 incentive, the world changed – the era of intercontinental air travel had begun.

This tradition of using incentives to revolutionise transport continues today in the form of the Go Fly Prize. Sponsored by Boeing, it offers a US$2 million award to the first team to make a quiet, light, personal flying device that can carry a single person 32 kilometres (20 miles). Teams from all over the world have banded together to work on their entries. The competition is in the prototyping stage and the prototypes so far are of all kinds – some resemble a motorcycle with 16 propellers, while others look like flying podiums with one or two rotors. Will we be flying around in these one day? The power of incentives says not to count it out.

Incentives can make incredible transformations not only at the technological frontier, but also in other areas where better outcomes are needed most. Like giving young people the best chance at a better life.

Middle schools in Washington, DC, are extremely disadvantaged. In a 2007 test, just 8 per cent of students were proficient in maths according to the national standard. So from 2008 to 2010 an experimental program was run in 34 heavily disadvantaged inner-city Washington, DC, schools. We're not talking stickers or extra recess. The program began *paying* students for completing tasks most of us would consider fundamental elements of school attendance. Students could receive money for showing up and for meeting behavioural standards, among other things. The average reward given to students was around US$44 every two weeks.

After two school years the results were clear. Grades went up. Behaviour improved. Student proficiency on the state mathematics test (which, granted, is considered more lenient than the national one referenced above) was 48.6 per cent for students who got the rewards compared to 41.6 per cent for those who did not.[1] In the context of education these results are substantial.

This incentive helped change grades and possibly lives. Somewhere out there a college graduate probably owes their academic trajectory to the bump they got from this program.

It's worth asking – should we be using incentives like these more often? Should we be applying them at every opportunity? Or is it somehow cheating?

If using rewards makes us feel like we're doing it wrong, we may be resigning ourselves to slower progress. The British Navy could have accepted shipwrecks as a price of sailing. The Washington, DC, education department could have accepted student failure as an insoluble problem. But in both cases they decided to push hard to get results.

This is one of the abiding truths I know about incentives: if you want to make things happen, you ought to harness their power. The –ology in the title of this book is there for a reason. Studying incentives carefully increases our chances of controlling them.

Careful study allows us to see patterns. When these patterns repeat we can make generalised observations. When these observations hold together cohesively we can call them theories.

I'm passionate about good theory, and this passion is shared by a man named Charlie Munger. Munger is a legend in the investing community and an autodidact when it comes to psychology. He started off working in a grocery store and went on to become a billionaire. (Munger is right-hand man to Warren Buffett at Berkshire Hathaway.) Said Munger in his speech 'The Psychology of Human Misjudgment',

> *I had always loved theory as an aid in puzzle solving and as a means of satisfying my monkey-like curiosity. And partly, I had found theory structure was a super-power in helping one get what one wanted.*[2]

Theories gift us understanding: seeing how a single example fits into a whole. Theories help us not only understand what we've already seen, but they also help us see more clearly. They work like a filter that helps us separate signal from noise when we look at the real world.

When you encounter incentives in the wild you want to be able to identify them, where they came from, how they work and how they fail. Without a functioning theory, doing so is much more difficult.

On incentives and human intellect

We humans are the smartest animals on earth. That's a pretty modest claim; our nearest competitors are probably apes, pigs or dolphins.

Yet for many centuries we had a solidly unimpressive collective track record at figuring out what was what. We believed in an ether, four humours and countless malevolent vapours.

Human 'knowledge' has a long- and well-established tendency to err. But we still have a few things going for us. The first is communication. We don't all need to figure stuff out separately; only one person has to, so long as they have the skills to communicate it to the rest of us, and people believe them. The second big advantage we've developed is the scientific process. Hypothesis testing with experimentation and data has helped us a lot. It has cleared the bramble fields of false belief in an extremely slow but hot-burning fire.

The scientific process has not made great inroads everywhere, though. Incentives are an abstract concept, and science is much further behind in the abstract fields (most humanities) than in the physical fields (most sciences). This is for a number of reasons:

- It's really easy to make mistakes in the abstract world.
- It's hard to test abstract concepts under laboratory conditions.
- Unlike a physical tool, an abstract idea doesn't make it clear when it stopped working.
- While physical tools endure, things that remain abstract get forgotten and warped.

What is a good abstract idea? It should exist not only as an idea you hold in your head, but as one I hold in mine, and one reflected on the page. It should be one everybody pretty much understands. Spreading these kinds of ideas can be very powerful.

Abstract ideas help build our social institutions. Parliament House is a building, but democracy is an abstraction. The jail in which you rot if you kill someone is physical, but the freedom we are denying you is an abstract idea. The reward you get for solving the longitude problem is concrete, but the promise of the incentive is abstract.

(The power of abstract ideas is why I'm a massive fan of not absolutely everyone getting their degrees in medicine or engineering. If some people could keep the flame of abstract human knowledge burning, that'd be great.)

Abstract ideas and theories shine a bright light on a world that would otherwise appear as an atomised series of absurd occurrences. But in the abstract world science has made relatively few steps. And where science has not trod, where no pre-existing answer has been found and communicated to us, our individual detective skills get to work.

This is not good. Not good at all.

The problem-solving human – eyebrows pulled low and tight; tongue slyly emerging like a worm after rain – generally relies on the 'thinking fast' skills described by Daniel Kahneman in his tremendous book, *Thinking, Fast and Slow*. Professor Kahneman's argument, if I may be so bold as to distil it, is that we think so fast we often miss the target.

In trying to explain something, the human mind can very swiftly formulate and propose a reason. Oftentimes that reason is very intuitive and appealing. Very often the reason sticks. Yet, intuitive and appealing reasons are often wrong.

One of the common mistakes humans make is called the fundamental attribution error. The fundamental attribution error is our tendency to attribute internal motivations as an explanation for why someone does something, rather than external motivations. This is a huge reason we fail to identify incentives – when we look for explanations for why a person does something, we look within that person rather than at their circumstances.

If you see someone driving like a maniac, you're more likely to mutter 'Arsehole!' than 'Probably a life or death situation has developed!' If you learn that a person lives in a rural area you might assume they like wide open spaces rather than guessing that property prices forced them out of the city. If someone doesn't take your calls you assume they're ignoring you rather than that they are visiting a friend in hospital, etc, etc.

The fundamental attribution error says we assume the explanation for behaviour is mostly in people's character rather than in the incentives they face. It explains why when someone triumphs we think they are brilliant and when someone fails we assume they didn't try hard enough. We rarely stop to think of the external factors that might explain what happened.

A great study on the phenomenon involved showing essays to a group of research participants and asking them to guess whether the author of the piece truly believed what the piece said. Essentially, it asked them to guess 'the true attitude' of the author. Most participants said they thought the author held the views put forth in the essay.

But the researchers did not expect what happened next. They told a second group of participants that the authors of the essay had been *instructed* to argue that position. Again the researchers asked the them whether the essay reflected the 'true attitude' of the author. And again they said they believed it did.

Even though they were specifically told external factors were at play, the participants chose to attribute what they saw to internal factors.

The fundamental attribution error is the subject of debate: how stable is it across cultures? Can we really call it an error when no explanation for individual human behaviour is ever fully provable? But these complaints don't undermine the central insight.

When we are aware of a bias we can start to correct it and in this way make space for a new theory. Knowing about the fundamental attribution error is the first step to understanding the importance of incentives.

A touch of humility

This book purports to explain a little about incentives, but before we really dive in it may be useful to ask: what is it to explain something?

Behind every observable phenomenon is another phenomenon. Normally more than one. For example, to explain television, you could explain the magic of radio waves. You could talk about the invention of the cathode ray tube. The remote control. The mysteries of plasma, LCD and LED screens. You could discuss the economics of the broadcast system and the contemporaneous development of free-to-air and broadcast stations. You could talk about humanity's love of storytelling and how television draws on a rich history of theatre and film.

The possibilities of explanation fan out behind any phenomenon you can name. Each explanation could itself prompt another dozen explanations. But then, if you trace any of these threads back far enough, they run out. They will collide with the limits of human knowledge or simply arrive back at the big bang.

The possibility space of explanations expands exponentially for the first few steps, but eventually collapses back down to our major knowns and unknowns. When we talk about explaining human behaviour by reference to incentives, we're grabbing just one of those threads. There are a million ways to explain any observable phenomenon on earth. The incentive system is only one.

It's important to remain humble about the relative power of an incentive-focused explanation versus the alternatives. This book does not advocate using incentives as the one-and-only all-powerful explanation for all things. If you're thinking about developing a theory for love or music or dancing based on incentives, I'd urge you to take a deep breath before you continue. The book is titled 'Incentivology', after all, not 'Incentivism'. Incentives are a tool – and an extremely powerful tool – but they're not a belief system.

Keeping the ball in the air

Earlier, you will recall, we hit pause with the ball frozen in midair. Let us proceed again.

As the ball succumbs to the relentless pull of gravity, I propel myself across the grass. I manoeuvre my body to where I expect the ball will land. Down down down comes the ball, while down down down I push my feelings of fear. I force my eyes to stay open, battling all the instincts that tell me to flinch. By the time the ball is approaching me, it's travelling fast. I stick my hands out, and, amazingly, the ball slams into them. It bobbles, but I clutch it against my chest. Safe! The ball is safe. I caught it!

Glee flows through my veins. My father looks happy, looks proud. We go back to the house and I hold the ball tightly the whole way. When we walk through the door my father tells my mother the story. He does not stint on emphasising how high the ball went. I beam.

'Go get a dollar from my bedside table,' he says. And I do, and when I grab it, it burns in my hand. I feel as though I earned this dollar more viscerally than any pocket money I might have got for doing chores.

I've remembered this episode my whole life. That day is etched into my brain. A lot of lessons might be drawn from it – about putting your fears aside, about achieving that which you thought you could not – but to me it's always been fundamentally about the power of incentives to make something happen that otherwise would not have.

Chapter 2

A Perverse Inclination

We've established what an incentive is, and that the power of incentives can be huge. But that fearsome energy is not like a laser, focused on its target. It spills over. Orteig's New York to Paris prize precipitated the demise of many an eager aviator. Incentives often have unintended consequences.

We commonly meet the term 'incentive' with the word 'perverse' preceding it. We *love* to hear about perverse incentives. Their symmetry pleases us – here's a scheme designed to do one thing that in fact achieves the opposite!

There are stories, for example, of pioneering palaeontologists paying peasants for any dinosaur bone fragments they found. The palaeontologists paid per piece. So when the local people found a big bone they would break it into smaller pieces, thereby destroying the huge finds that would have been invaluable to the palaeontologists. Likewise, when drivers in China were obliged to pay the medical bills of anyone they injured while driving, there were stories of cars clipping pedestrians and then reversing over them, because funerals were cheaper than hospital bills.

Such stories are always circulating, because they're exactly the sort of ironic reversal that seems to delight us. But attempting to verify them can be an exercise in frustration. Many seem to be urban legends. They live on in retelling because they work for us; a good story of a perverse incentive is like a Greek tragedy in one simple anecdote – it shows the mighty coming unstuck in their hubristic plans to control the world.

A French reversal

To see a terrific (and true) perverse incentive in action I want to take you back in time again to what was then known as French Indochina.

In 1890 in the city of Ha Noi, Vietnam, there was a vermin problem. Rats. The common mammalian pest had always been present in Ha Noi, but the French, bringing with them all the wisdom of Europe, had embarked on a project to construct sewers beneath the city as part of their mission to spread 'civilisation' to South-East Asia (and of course gain access to valuable markets, but *shhh*). The march of progress – *naturellement* – began in the European quarter. Sewers connected each French mansion and channelled their waste away.

Such feats of engineering in the service of hygiene appeared to be the height of modernity. But there was a hiccup. For the rats, this French colonial project was all upside. In the stinky tunnels beneath the colonialists' homes, they raised offspring in unprecedented numbers. A rat plague descended on Ha Noi, and its epicentre was the European quarter. Streets and homes alike began to crawl with bold brown rats.

As the twentieth century dawned, the germ theory of disease was in ascendance, pushing aside the idea that disease was carried in miasmas or vapours. The epidemics of cholera, typhus and yellow fever that tore through urban populations in the previous century now had an explanation, and the French were at the forefront of developing that explanation. When several cases of bubonic plague were recorded in Ha Noi the focus on rats sharpened.

The French wanted the rats gone. Now. At least from the *quartier européen*.

They hired Vietnamese workers to hunt rats, and paid them the equivalent of about US$0.02 per rat killed ($US0.60 in 2019 dollars). Colonial records show the system was immediately effective. One thousand rats died per day in the first week of May 1902. To avoid rat corpses piling up too high the French demanded only the rat tails as proof. It was a simple rule – money for tails.

By mid May, the number of tails presented rose to over 4000 a day. This evidently made hardly a dent in the sewer populations, because by the end of May, as the superior brain of the *Homo sapiens* trained itself in the pursuit of rodents, the number of rat tails the French were paying for per day hit 15,000.[1]

At this point the French may have started to wonder if their incentive was just a little bit too good. The bounty on the tail of each rat fell by a quarter.

The details of this story come to us via a wonderful historian named Michael Vann. He obtained all the necessary permits to enter the Vietnamese national archives and trawled through the extremely detailed records left by the French colonial administrations. Professor Vann has endured the slings and arrows of being 'the sewer historian' and at one point he was even bitten by a rat in the colonial archives. But luckily for us he persevered.

According to documents found by Professor Vann in the archives, the rat tails being collected were as various as they were bountiful. The rat hunters claimed they were hunting all rats – including those that had not grown to their full adult size. The French paid out for *les grandes* and *les petites*. But they began to suspect mouse, vole and other tails were polluting the daily collections.

Furthermore, as the supply of rat tails went on and on and on, officials began to wonder if rats were being imported from villages surrounding Ha Noi to claim the bounty. (They likely were.)

Final confirmation the system was being gamed came when a French bureaucrat checking up on things in central Ha Noi stumbled on something he was not supposed to see: a rat farm. Chasing wild rats is hard. Why bother going down into the filthy sewers when, using the exponentially increasing magic of breeding, you could grow your own? The incentive designed to reduce the number of rats in Ha Noi was paradoxically and perversely encouraging rat breeding.

In late 1902 the French shut their disastrous incentive system down, and the rat farms lost their *raison d'être*. It is unknown what happened to the farmed rats, but it is certainly easy to imagine the doors of those cages being thrown open and the rats scampering out. In 1903 the plague came to Ha Noi and the worst fears of its administrators were realised.

This story has it all – a beautiful tango between administrative arrogance and human ingenuity that ends in disaster. I particularly love the metaphor of the French building their sewers. They think they are setting up an efficient and contemporary system to take a problem away. But at the same time they are creating a subterranean point of entry for a whole new problem, in this case rats and disease. This metaphor is one we will see repeated: whenever we create a new system we provide a pipeline for something quite unexpected to come along and bite us.

A bird in the hand

I love history, but in using an example from long ago there is a risk. We may imagine the mistake has been eliminated, just as we eliminated plague, smallpox and polio. Ha! In our richly governed modern life, incentive systems that drive absurd and counter-productive behaviour are everywhere. Perverse incentives thrive like rats in French sewers.

A terrific example can be found not in rats but in Birds.

Bird is an electric scooter sharing scheme. It deploys kick scooters, not unlike the ones you see children riding, but powered by a large battery. Perhaps by the time you read this, the electric scooter is a workaday part of the urban fabric and it's hard to imagine a time before them. Alternatively, perhaps the electric scooter has gone the way of the Segway before it. But at time of writing, their future is unclear.

Hoping to find the next Uber, many American venture capitalists are striving to win market share in the transport industry. They are throwing money at the entrepreneurs who believe electric scooters are the next big thing. Set up a scooter-sharing network large enough and dominance of the industry will follow, the venture capitalists assume.

But the scooter-sharing industry has problems. Unlike a ride-share car, which has a driver, scooters are abandoned at their destinations. There is nobody to recharge them or defend them against vandalism. And once their batteries run down, the scooters are kaput. Someone needs to go get them and plug them in.

To solve this problem, Bird pays people to collect scooters at night, take them back to their homes and plug them in to charge, then put them back on the streets in the morning. Collecting and charging a scooter earns you US$5. Bird has had little trouble getting the scooters charged; people seem willing to collect a bit of money for doing the job.

Some scooters get left on main streets, so they're easy to collect. But others get left in odd places. Down a dark alleyway. On private property. These scooters don't get collected so easily – the

$5 payment for collecting them is not worth it. Over time, more and more scooters end up in strange and hard-to-reach locations, and that means fewer scooters in circulation.

So Bird has a system. If a scooter is left abandoned for a couple of days, it's obviously one that's hard to collect – so the payment for collecting it goes up. The scooter collectors can make $20 instead of $5 for it. Can you see how to abuse this system?

The answer is to take a scooter and hide it. Put it somewhere where other people can't collect it, but you can access it any time. Once the fee for collecting it has risen, you mark it as found and plug it in.[2]

The incentive designed to keep scooters *in* circulation has the perverse effect of taking them *out of* circulation. It's a classic case of a perverse incentive. The French wanted fewer rats on the streets; they got more. Bird wanted more scooters on the streets; they got fewer.

There are incentives that achieve their goals. Then there are incentives that cause surprise side effects. An incentive that directly undermines itself is a special subset of this latter case, where the surprise side effects run directly counter to the intended goal.

Goodhart's Law

Perverse incentives are an example of a general principle: the tendency of attempts at control to fall apart. For economists, this truth is captured by a well known aphorism named Goodhart's Law.

Charles Goodhart, a British economist, was concerned about monetary policy – those actions taken by central banks to control economic growth, inflation and money supply. Relationships between the various measures were clear in the data – when one went up, the other went down, etc. What made Goodhart frown was that when the government grabbed the controls that drove monetary policy, they promptly became wobbly.

'Any observed statistical regularity will tend to collapse once pressure is placed upon it for control purposes,' Goodhart observed.[3] (He named this observation Goodhart's Law, in what appears to have been a throwaway joke. In accordance with Murphy's Law, it became his most famous intellectual legacy.)

You may also be aware of a very similar observation, known as the Lucas Critique, by another famous economist. Goodhart's Law and the Lucas Critique have their origins in different parts of economic theory but for our purposes the pair carry the same warning: those who try to control outcomes will tend to get surprised. We'll discuss the Lucas Critique in a bit more detail in Chapter 11.

We can see Goodhart's Law in action whenever incentives turn perverse. The observed (or assumed) statistical regularity – that each rat tail brought in would equate to one less rat running wild in Ha Noi – collapsed when it was used for control. Likewise the assumption that any uncollected scooter must be out of reach of a scooter collector.

When patents were invented to encourage people to invest in creating new ideas, nobody imagined patent trolls who would buy up patents and sue anybody who tried to use the ideas – ideas they didn't even develop. But the perverse incentive of patents is to make this business model – one that inhibits the use of new ideas – viable.

Likewise, when American fuel economy standards were made, nobody imagined they would impede improvements in fuel economy. But the fuel standards had a strange effect – they made cars bigger.

Of course, you can't expect a large vehicle and a small vehicle to use the same amount of fuel. So the law ensured limits were higher for larger cars. It turned out to be more profitable for manufacturers to make and sell larger vehicles that met lower standards, and they did so with gusto. The perverse result was more large vehicles on

US roads consuming more fuel and emitting more carbon dioxide. The top-selling vehicle in the US is now the Ford F-Series, a giant beast of a thing, that gets fuel economy of 20 miles per gallon (12L/100km). The second and third best-sellers are basically the same kind of vehicle with different badges on the grille.[4]

Unexpected and perverse outcomes are almost inevitable whenever someone sets out to harness the power of incentives. If a small group of people designs an incentive for a large group of people, you can be confident the larger group will work out how to exploit it. No matter how many PhDs the designers may have, the power of the incentive will drive the masses to figure out an unanticipated way to game the system. This is the great bargain one must accept in using incentives. No power comes for free. The cost of using incentives is that you will forever be compelled to watch for the surprising effects they have.

However, remember the parable of the French. Their incentive scheme was being exploited. But when they abandoned it, rats returned in seething masses, and not long afterward the plague arrived in Ha Noi. The goal in identifying perverse outcomes is not to create such despair that designers abandon their incentive schemes. Instead they should tweak the rules, wait and watch, and tweak again.

Chapter 3

Unintentional

When I set out to write this book, several of my friends tried to help me by explaining the bonus systems that operate at their workplaces. I listened attentively and I learned a lot. The biggest lesson I learned was that when people think about incentives what comes to mind is a system wearing a nametag that says, 'Hello, I am an incentive.' But some incentives are camouflaged and escape our notice.

We recognise incentives most easily in the workplace. I blame Chester Barnard. The grandfather of modern incentive theory, Barnard elaborated his ideas in a 1938 book called *The Functions of the Executive*. Barnard put incentives into the workplace context and they've been struggling to break out ever since. But it is outside the workplace that incentives are most interesting.

A lot of brilliant work has been done by academics on incentive systems. But a huge proportion of it has been on the 'principal–agent relationship' problem.

The principal–agent relationship is about two people, where one is trying to get the other to do something. The principal designs an incentive and the agent essentially tries to figure out how to get the reward while doing the bare minimum. It's great for understanding employer–employee situations and how people behave when we pay them to do things – including literal agents, like travel agents and real estate agents.

The problem with this analysis is not its content but its central assumption: that there exists a principal – a person – designing an incentive scheme. I contend that many incentive systems have no particular principal. Or, if they do, that entity did not realise they were designing an incentive scheme. Or, if that entity *was* trying to make an incentive scheme, they also made a bunch of other ones by mistake.

If incentives can come into existence as a side effect of some other decision, the implication is that there is rarely a watchful eye or a hand on the tiller to correct them when they are going wrong. Does this sound alarming? It should.

One of the most abundant kinds of incentive is the accidental incentive. As the name suggests, these are created by mistake and are generally a side effect of some other endeavour. Unlike perverse incentives – which are a subset of accidental incentive – most accidental or unintentional incentives don't impinge on the main goal of the incentive. Instead they affect something else entirely.

A terrific example of an accidental incentive is the effect of school zones. School zones are common around the world: geographic areas around public schools that ensure any school-aged child living within those areas will be accepted into those schools.

I live in the Australian state of Victoria. The state department of education here proclaims school zones exist 'to ensure students have access to neighbourhood schools'. The policy guidelines suggest it's about access to something convenient: 'The closest school is measured by a straight line from your permanent address. Or it is measured by the shortest practical route. This may consider roads and travel time.'[1]

This seems like a practical measure. School zones also help manage demand for public schools so that the department of education knows how many classrooms and teachers it needs in each school. All sounds appropriate and simple enough.

But school zones can create an accidental incentive effect. Why? Because not all public schools are created equal. Students at some seem to get far better results on average, and parents want those better results for their children. They can set you up for life. In Victoria, results from high school determine which courses you may study, and at which university. The parents whose deepest aspiration is that their child will get into a hotly demanded course at a well-reputed university want, nay, *need* the child to get good results in high school.

If there is a public school that holds out the promise of sparkling results, a university education that commands respect and the ensuing lifetime of success, it's Balwyn High. Alumni include surgeons, professors, top lawyers, and so on. Come December, students from Balwyn High crowd the top of the rankings. In 2018 one student nabbed a coveted perfect score of 99.95 – awarded to just 0.05 per cent of all students in the state of Victoria. Around 16 per cent of students from Balwyn High School got results in the top 3 per cent of the state.[2] Balwyn High School's results are very good indeed. Most of the other schools that achieve results like this are either very expensive private schools, or public schools that offer selective entrance via exams. Balwyn High is different. It's just a local school, drawing on a local school zone like any other.

People with kids want to move into that school zone. Desperately. Census data confirms Balwyn and Balwyn North – the suburbs in which the Balwyn High school zone falls – are disproportionately full of high-school-aged children. In Balwyn North, children aged between 10 and 19 comprise around 9 per cent of the population, compared to a state and national average of 6 per cent. In the neighbouring suburb of Kew – which does not have a celebrated public high school – around 6.5 per cent of the population is 10 to 19 year olds.[3]

This extra demand for property among the parents of school-aged children shows up in property prices. Let us look at two houses, alike in dignity (and both for sale at time of writing). Both are in Balwyn North. Both have three bedrooms, one bathroom and two parking spaces. One sits on 650 square metres of land; the other sits on 697 square metres. There is no significant difference between the interiors or exteriors, but the slightly smaller block is advertised for $1.55 million, while the slightly larger block is advertised for $1.35 million. The reason for the substantial price discrepancy? The vicissitudes of school zoning. The first house is in the Balwyn High school zone while the second falls just outside it.

This kind of price differential is similar to what we see in the data overall. According to analysis by the Real Estate Institute of Victoria, houses in the Balwyn High zone cost more than those just bordering the zone by $142,500.[4] The principal of the successful school has joked publicly that she can no longer afford to live in the area.[5]

The school zone runs down the middle of some streets in Balwyn, and takes some cruel zigzags that exclude houses from the zone. People who own houses on the lucky side get access to something worth over one hundred thousand dollars. Those on the other side miss out.

Higher home prices are not the only effect. Development is also filling in this traditionally low-rise suburb. Just inside the school zone's western edge now stands a multistorey apartment block. Some old blocks of land were merged and now host 35 apartments. How many of these apartments will be filled with families with school-aged children? The name of the development provides a clue: it's called Balwyn High Apartments (although entirely unassociated with the school, mind you).

In 2018, several two-bedroom apartments in the Balwyn High Apartments development were snapped up, one for $738,000. I wanted to find a new two-bedroom apartment just outside the zone to illustrate for you the premium for apartments inside the school zone. But, tellingly, there aren't any new apartments just outside the zone to compare to. Developers seem uncannily eager to work inside the school zone.

The Balwyn High school zone is not designed as a subsidy for living in the zone – but it operates like one. And it is not meant to encourage higher density development – but it works to do that too. None of this was in the brief when the Department of Education set out to rationally allocate students to schools. It's all unintentional.

A school zone is about who goes to school where, but it's an example of a bigger kind of question – who gets what? It turns out that when we create rules to answer that question, we tend to create accidental incentive schemes. Whether we allocate things by location, citizenship, employment status, connections or ready cash, we have a disconcerting tendency to create accidental incentives – like 'greencard marriages' to get US citizenship or camping out overnight to get tickets to a concert. Some are more inclined to perverse outcomes than others, but all can make people do strange things. Things the people who created the system have no incentive to encourage – and may have little incentive to discourage either. This is how our world fills up with accidental incentives.

Doing it for the 'gram

At 1.26 pm on 16 July 2010 a man named Mike Krieger uploaded the first ever photo to the photo-sharing service that would soon become known as Instagram. Krieger, who wrote the code for that service, later sold Instagram to Facebook and became very, very rich.

But at the time he was just your average nerd. Krieger's first photo was a badly framed landscape, but two and a half hours later he changed the world forever when he posted the first ever Instagram food shot.

You can still find that photo online. It doesn't pass muster by today's standards – it's dark and blurry and taken at the end of a Vietnamese meal when things are a mess. The choice of filter is highly questionable. And yet it stands as a turning point in culinary history. It has changed the way chefs work and the way we eat.

Instagram was launched as a place for people to share the photographs they had taken. You set up an account and by default anyone on the whole internet can follow you and see your photos. They can like them and comment beneath. The big idea of Instagram in the early days was 'filters', which added different colour and shading effects to photographs. Instagram hoped to change the way photos looked.

They certainly did that. But they also quite accidentally managed to change the way the world looks. Nowhere is this more visible than when you go out to eat. Food has subtly changed. Restaurants whose dishes are shared online gain free marketing, with the promise of new customers, while those whose dishes never grace social media must work twice as hard to keep up.

As a result, meals at fashionable places now pop with colour and symmetry. They must be plated up with precision. They dazzle visually. Stews and mushroom soups? Too brown. Mashed potatoes and scrambled eggs? Too sloppy. It's a great era for colourful fruits and shapely vegetables. Boring meats are arrayed artfully and accompanied by elaborate garnishes or bright sauces.

I remember when I first realised how important visual presentation had become for food. I ordered a serve of nachos at a fashionable brunch spot. Nachos are famously messy, but not this time. The plate came out looking sculptural. Atop the gleaming pile of guacamole and artfully scattered tortilla chips, a large circle of candied orange was perched vertically. It was so surprising and stunning, I immediately reached for my phone to take a photo. As I did so another meal was placed on the table, more beautiful than the last. I gasped, at first in awe and then in realisation.

Opening Instagram and seeing the restaurant's account only confirmed it – this was strategy. (The strategy requires not only aesthetic brilliance but continual innovation. A slice of orange is no longer enough to compete in the Instagram marketplace; since I was there, Instagram reveals this brunch spot has begun serving eggs benedict on the blade of a shovel instead of a plate, and a sandwich with a syringe of smashed avocado inserted in it.)

Chefs have always cooked for our eyes as well as our stomachs. The two needs were in balance so long as restaurants relied on word of mouth. Now the marketing reach of visual impact is far greater than the reach of flavour. At fashionable restaurants – the kind that rely on Instagram to refill the lines of patiently waiting customers that snake round the block – the need for dishes to be beautiful has streaked ahead.

Of course dishes can't taste bad if a restaurant is to be successful. And of course a local restaurant with a loyal clientele can retain a terrific following with humbler-looking offerings. But until someone can invent an app that shares flavours it will remain extremely challenging to go viral with a delicious but ugly meal.

Instagram is increasingly part of the recipe for restaurant success no matter how big or small you are. In 2014 the US fast food chain Chilli's did a full marketing refresh. One of its big decisions was to spend hundreds of thousands of dollars each year on a flavourless glaze to put on its burger buns so they would glisten better in photos.

Restaurants' fever for Instagram success also means styling has gone beyond the food. One San Francisco champagne bar, The Riddler, is especially Instagram savvy. It offers a panoply of quirky menu options that pop up on Instagram time and again. The 'chambong' is a good example, described on the menu as 'a bong of bubbles. Yes this is a thing.' (It functions the same way as a beer bong – it's a champagne flute with a tube at the bottom to drink from.)

It's not just the menu options that are instagrammable at The Riddler: a simpler and even more instagrammable feature is the table reservations. When tables are reserved, the signs have celebrity names on them: 'Reserved for Oprah', 'Reserved for Lady Gaga', etc. To judge by the volume of Instagram posts, this simple addition to the dining space is a thunderbolt of marketing genius.

The word 'instagrammable' barely even existed prior to 2015. Now it's the difference between success and failure for a whole subset of restaurants. There's growing evidence that chefs invent dishes with photography in mind, and the trend is placing flavour at risk. The blog of the esteemed Auguste Escoffier School of Culinary Arts in the US now feels it necessary to provide tips on how to 'Create Instagram-Worthy Plates That Aren't Staged Or Flavorless'.

Did Instagram really change the world?

Hardware aficionados could take issue with the above analysis. They might say that the ubiquity of high-quality photography has driven the change described, that putting a camera in every pocket is the swing factor. That's true enough – without phone cameras there would be no Instagram. But it's an overly simple analysis that takes the human out of the picture: cameras don't share photos alone. While the lenses and light sensors made the app possible, it's humans who take and share food photos. Why? Because incentives affect humans, not hardware.

The attention that accrues to Instagram photos is valuable because we are a social species. We generally crave the recognition and love of others. As anyone who has an Instagram account knows, when you see a beautiful scene it isn't long before you think of photographing it, and once you've snapped a photo it isn't long before you think of sharing it.

The primary incentive provided by Instagram is intentional – to take and share beautiful photos. The second-round effect – that the restaurant business becomes a much more visual one – is entirely accidental.

This particular accidental incentive is mostly good. The contrarian view is easy to find – chefs pine for an imaginary past when diners cared only about flavour. And, sure, a few dishes may have suffered flavour-wise, just like a few San Francisco nights have surely gone haywire after one too many chambongs. But mostly the incentives created for restaurants by Instagram are benign – they encourage the industry to create an environment that is more visually delightful.

The accidental incentives created by Instagram in other domains, meanwhile, are different – the high flow of rewarding likes for selfies taken on cliff edges, for example, contributes not only to increased erosion of delicate landscapes but also to frequent death by misadventure.

Whenever a system is created that relies on human interaction or human emotions, incentives change. If the system is big and powerful enough, then even the most subtle change in incentives can aggregate into a powerful behaviour change.

Chapter 4

Missing Incentives

Incentives can go horribly wrong, as we've discussed. One instinct upon hearing all this might be to give up on them altogether and hope to rely on our better natures. But that could be an even bigger mistake. Some of the most monstrous disasters happen when incentives are omitted.

Take the release of pollution into rivers. When there is no incentive to not dump it, waterways run thick with filth. Or financial advice – when advisors are not prohibited from recommending their own products, they can make their clients much worse off.

These are very important topics. But they lack for duels, leg irons and icebergs. I'd like to tell a story of missing incentives that has all those and more.

A tale of two Marys

We start in Covent Garden Market, around 3 am on an early summer's morning in August 1789 – mild, so far as London goes. Stallholders were laying out their produce, getting ready for customers to flood through around dawn, when two outsiders wandered in. Mary Butler and Mary Desmond, poor Irish immigrants in London.

'We had been at a labour, and went to get some drink,' Mary Butler said later.[1]

It's not clear why the two ladies gave up their plan for a beverage. Did they see what happened next as a gleeful escapade? Or was it a crime committed in desperate economic need?

Encountering the stall of one Amelia Read, the two Irishwomen grabbed a large basket full of 9 pecks of French beans and legged it. (A French bean is just a green bean. A peck is about 9 litres, so 9 pecks is 81 litres. I recommend visualising as many beans as you could fit in a hotel bar-fridge, i.e. a heck of a lot of beans.) Before they got far they were spotted.

Mary and Mary mounted their own defence in court, insisting they were framed by a person with a grudge, and Mary Butler called five character witnesses to testify in her defence, but when Amelia Read told the court that she had lost 9 pecks of beans in a wicker basket that night, the case was pretty much up.

1789 was a bad time to be convicted in the British courts. When America won independence from Britain the government of George III had tried to keep sending convicts for a while, but the Americans kept sending them back. Luckily Britain had found a new place to send its unwanted. The first fleet of British convict ships had arrived to colonise Australia in 1788.

As the ships wended their way back to England, the government was counting the cost of the First Fleet and planning a second. The number of convicts aboard would be higher the second time round, the government decided, and the cost of the trip would have to be far less. The British Admiralty planned to put the job out to tender and choose the lowest bidder.

Sending convicts to Australia far outweighed the cost of the crime. The value of the beans in the case above was 4 shillings sixpence (£33 in today's British pounds) and the basket worth

2 shillings (£15). That was £48 of crime in contemporary terms, or around £24 per Mary.

To punish the perpetrators the government of England would pay a sum more than 50 times that (£17, 7 shillings and sixpence, equivalent to £2500[2]) to a transport company to load Mary Desmond and Mary Butler on a ship bound for Australia, called the *Neptune*.[3]

Embarking aboard the *Neptune* with Mary Desmond and Mary Butler was Thomas Barnett, sentenced to transportation for stealing 20 yards of silk ribbon, Thomas Bateman, for stealing silk handkerchiefs, and Martha Bates, for stealing a child's linen shift. As a school student in Australia you hear a lot about convicts getting transportation for stealing a loaf of bread. Far more of them appear to have robbed a haberdashery.

(In 1789 cloth was very expensive, although about to begin a great price depreciation – the industrial revolution has only just brought into existence the cotton-spinning machine, and not yet the loom. Wool, muslin, linen and silk truly were the iPads of the day: expensive, desirable, and as easy to fence as to swipe. A truly astonishing proportion of the criminals aboard the *Neptune* had stolen clothing or fabric. One starts to understand why Dickens's pickpockets were always after handkerchiefs.)

When Mary Desmond and Mary Butler and all the rest clank up the gangplank onto the *Neptune*, it has not yet sailed its way into infamy. But inside the government, one senior admiralty official had already raised a warning.

Britain's experience with exporting convicts was already long; they'd been sending them to America for years with few problems. Convict ships on the Atlantic route would keep their cargo alive, because the convicts wouldn't sell for much otherwise. But when convicts arrived in Australia, by contrast, they would automatically be the responsibility of the colonial governor, so the captains of the transport ships didn't need to sell them to anyone. Sir Charles Middleton – a bureaucrat with a keen sense for the importance of incentives – could see that Britain's experience in taking convicts to America might not apply when convicts were being shipped to Australia.

'[T]he merchants who had taken convicts to America had an interest in them after they were embarked,' wrote Middleton in 1786. While on the voyage to Australia they had 'no other advantage but the freight and the victualling, and take the risk of their Ships ... upon themselves'.[4]

What Middleton could see, that few others did, was that those who won the contracts to ship convicts to Australia had no financial motivations to care for them.

This warning would come to seem prophetic. The 502 convicts loaded aboard the *Neptune* – 424 men and 78 women – paid a heavy price for that missing incentive. But at the time, nobody was interested.

The hellship *Neptune*

The winning bidder for the Second Fleet contract was Camden, Calvert and King, a very successful old slave-trading company that, having lost its business across the Atlantic, was making an agile pivot to carrying convicts to the Antipodes. The *Neptune* sailed in a fleet of three, alongside the *Scarborough* and the *Surprize*, from London on 19 January 1790. Trouble began before the ships had even made it to the ocean.

We are on the docks outside the Fountain Tavern in Plymouth where a crowd has gathered, hushed expectantly. Two men stand back-to-back. Upon the signal they begin: ten deliberate strides before turning and pulling the triggers on their long-barrelled pistols.

The two men are John Macarthur, an officer of the New South Wales Corps, and Thomas Gilbert: captain of the *Neptune*, veteran of the First Fleet, and employee of Camden, Calvert and King.

Both Macarthur and Gilbert survived the duel, likely to the disappointment of the dispersing crowd but not to their surprise – the incentive to agree to a duel would change very rapidly later when guns that shot straight were invented.

Why did they fight? Macarthur and his wife were unhappy about conditions aboard. Stomach infections among the convicts were already rampant – remember, Plymouth was only the last stop in England before they plunged down through the Atlantic. Several convicts had died below decks already, despite the mostly estuarine journey so far. Macarthur wanted, not unreasonably, someone to clean up the shit. The captain seemed disposed to leave the hundreds of unfortunates chained together below decks to wallow in it.

Complaints about harsh treatment of convicts seemed justified. William Hill, a captain in the NSW Corps aboard the *Surprize*, wrote in a letter home about what he saw on the *Neptune*:

> *The irons used upon these unhappy wretches were barbarous … they could not extend either leg from the other more than an inch or two at most; thus fettered, it was impossible for them to move, but at the risk of both their legs being broken.*[5]

After the duel the slave-trading company swapped Captain Gilbert out for a new one, Donald Trail. (Macarthur and his wife eventually transferred to another ship in the fleet and went on to pioneer the Australian wool industry and instigate the 1808 Rum Rebellion to overthrow the governor of the colony.)

But the arrangements under Captain Trail appear to have remained unchanged: not only was there no bonus payment for keeping his new charges alive, but there was also a rule that said any unused provisions aboard the boat could be sold upon arrival in Australia (on top of the contractual reserve provided for the successful delivery of stores to the new colony). This was an exceedingly dangerous combination. Fewer mouths to feed would leave more provisions unused.

Would a captain really starve the convicts? In his letter, Captain Hill implied such a plan existed.

The slave trade is merciful compared to what I have seen in this fleet … In this fleet, the more they can withhold from the unhappy wretches, the more provisions they have to dispose of in a foreign market; and the earlier in the voyage they die, the longer they can draw the deceased's allowance for themselves.

If Captain Trail was starving the convicts – and multiple sources attest to it – it is in part because selling leftover food and goods to the people of Sydney upon his arrival would be lucrative. The colony was starved for goods. They had not had a supply ship since the First Fleet. And thanks to an awfully northerly iceberg, they would not have one again for some time.

A store ship, *Guardian*, left London ahead of the convict ships only to hit an iceberg near the southern tip of Africa. It only just limped to shore at Cape Town. When the *Neptune* pulled in a little later the crew of the *Guardian* were eager to hand off the stores bound for Australia, but the captain of the *Neptune* seemed surprisingly unwilling to take on board any of the stores. Those were not stores they could sell, you see. Those were stores that belonged to the colony and would compete with the goods Trail hoped to sell.

Of course, a convict ship would always expect a few deaths. Sea travel was very dangerous. The British Navy assumed a death rate of 1 in 30 whenever it went to sea during the Napoleonic wars – and that's without any battle casualties. Those trips were just short jaunts compared to travel to the continent of Australia. The First Fleet set sail without knowing if it would make it at all. By the time it arrived in Port Jackson, 48 funerals had been held at sea, leaving the convict death rate at approximately 5 per cent. Those losses were costly. While these criminals were detested in England, taking up increasingly scarce space in the jails, they were crucial to the development of England's new colony in Australia. Convicts were labour.

In total the *Neptune* would spend 159 days at sea, killing an estimated 150 of its 502 convicts along the way. Upon arrival in Australia, some 350 were still living. Just. Many of those would die soon after arrival. The First Fleet chaplain Richard Johnson depicts the state of the convicts upon their arrival:

> *I beheld a sight truly shocking to the feelings of humanity, a great number of them laying, some half, others nearly quite naked, without either bed or bedding, unable to turn or help themselves. Spoke to them as I passed along, but the smell was so offensive that I could scarcely bear it … The landing of these people was truly affecting and shocking; great numbers were not able to walk, nor to move hand or foot; such were slung over the ship side in the same manner as they would a cask, a box, or anything of that nature. Upon their being brought up to the open air some fainted, some died upon deck, and others in the boat before they reached the shore.*[6]

Note that the shocked author of this description himself had arrived in Australia on a convict ship just two years earlier. He was hardly unaware of the usual hazards of sea travel. But the incentives on the Second Fleet were far more dangerous than was usual. While the *Neptune* had the highest death rate of nearly one third, the other two ships in the fleet saw mortality rates of 15–30 per cent. And the death did not stop upon arrival. If you measure survival within eight months of arrival in Sydney, the mortality rate of Second Fleet convicts was 40 per cent.[7]

The slightly higher survival aboard the *Scarborough* and the *Surprize* suggests that no matter how powerful they may be, the presence or absence of external incentives is not the be all and end all. While incentives agitate neural networks of reward (more on this in Chapter 6), those neural networks will nevertheless operate in the absence of incentives. Morals do exist. Absent a good contract, the only force that could have kept convicts in better shape was the conscience of the captain, and the captains of the other two ships in the fleet succeeded in killing fewer of their charges than Captain Trail, despite the same incentives being in operation.

Clearly, the incentives of the Second Fleet were a disaster. The £17, 7 shillings and sixpence paid to the slave traders per convict needed to have some component reserved for successful delivery of cargo. The sad thing was that the contract included such a reserve for the successful delivery of stores, including rations and clothes, hammers and nails. But there was no such reserve for the people. Trail could have thrown all the convicts into the sea just off Penzance and collected his money. (Perhaps that happened to some of them. Records do not show where or when in the journey convicts died.)

And what of the two Marys? Surely one made it at least? I'm pleased to report both Ms Butler and Ms Desmond arrived in Sydney alive, and both promptly married (which is another story – there were 529 men on the First Fleet and a paltry 188 women, so the Second Fleet, while still only carrying roughly 300 women to 850-odd men, was welcomed with open arms by the male population).

Lash and backlash

What is encouraging about the Second Fleet is the response. Once news of the death rate and inhuman conditions on board began to filter back to Britain, the newspapers of London frothed with news of the horrors of the journey. Terrible stories were told of men chained together: when one died the other would feign for as long as possible that the man at the other end of the iron links was still alive in order to claim his rations. Amid these lurid stories, the *Times of London* made a fascinating suggestion: pay attention to incentives.

> *It may be proper to observe that the sum allowed by government for each convict to Botany Bay is fully adequate – but it unfortunately happens that the owners farm the business to the Master of the ship and therefore the more that die on the passage, the greater his gains. The bill of lading should be in the usual style 'to deliver the cargo in the like good order and well conditioned as aforesaid, (the danger of the seas only excepted).' But as the matter now stands, the less of his cargo the Captain brings into Port, the more profit he makes.*[8]

I love this. It was part of a shift in public opinion that helped effect change in the system of transportation forever. The next ships to sail would do so under a very simple system: cash on delivery. Contractors would be paid only for each pair of convict feet that walked off the ship in Sydney. How did this incentive go? I present a letter from the lieutenant governor of the colony back to his masters on 12 October 1793:

> *The contractor ... appears to have performed his engagement with great liberality; and the prisoners they have conveyed prove by their healthy appearance the extraordinary attention that must have been*

paid by the Naval Agents. In two ships containing three hundred and three people, one person only had died, and amongst those landed in the colony scarcely any are sick.[9]

(The one death was an alleged mutineer, executed just six weeks after they left Europe. That's a different kind of incentive system in operation – one designed to keep order.)

Did this simple system continue to work? Ultimately no: it didn't account for some risks that were truly out of the hands of the transport company. For example, if a convict was brought aboard with a virulent fever, many could die despite their best efforts. A better balance of risk and reward was required, and it turned out better results could be gained with a more nuanced system. Britain experimented for a while with a mixture of bonuses and direct accountability that proved ideal, and the death rates for the journey to Australia fell to around 1 per cent.[10] What was necessary to solve a huge problem was not a huge incentive to do the right thing. Just that one existed at all.

As our societies tackle the problems of climate change and plastics choking the ocean, this example should give us hope. A few well-placed incentives can make a big difference to a seemingly disastrous problem.

Chapter 5

Your Brain on Incentives

To fully understand incentives we need to not only understand *what* they do but *why*. We must dive deeper into the underlying causes that make humans respond to incentives, and that means looking into our brain's reward system. This is the system that makes us seek certain things in life – food, water, and, ahem, etc – and makes them feel so good.

The basic science of the reward system is familiar to many of us these days. We generally understand that our desires, dreams and feelings of accomplishment are nothing more than evanescent chemical signals sparkling across the pale grey sludge of our brains.

But as recently as the 1940s, such a concept was not common knowledge. Around the middle of the last century neuroscientists made big advances by studying people with brain injuries to work out the role of the brain in motivation. Some people with physical changes in their brain stopped eating. Others would not *stop* eating. A scientific revolution was afoot. Scientists began to realise it was not the stomach that made a person hungry, nor the throat that made a person thirsty. The brain was central to it all. Like much knowledge we now take for granted, the idea that motivation is located in the brain was once an insight.

And the true turning point in discovering the role of the brain in motivation required a clumsy and undertrained young man called James Olds.

Remote control

In 1953 James Olds got a job at a laboratory at Canada's McGill University. He was working over the summer that year, determined to impress his superiors with what he had discovered while they were relaxing. Olds had a bunch of rats he could use, and he began to experiment.

Rat brains are tiny. When you introduce an electrode, it's easy to miss your intended target, especially if you don't have an experienced hand – and Olds's hands were still young. With one unfortunate rat he blazed right past the mid-brain reticular system and plunged straight into the rhinencephalic nerve.

A more fortuitous mistake has rarely been made in neuroscience. Olds promptly discovered he had created a rat he could remote control.

To begin the experiment, Olds placed the rat in a box with four corners marked A, B, C and D. When the rat went to corner A it got an electric stimulation to its brain, right in the rhinencephalic nerve. The rat returned to corner A time and again. Wrote Olds, 'At this point we assumed that the stimulus must provoke curiosity; we did not yet think of it as a reward.'[1]

The rat soon fell asleep, but the next day it went back to corner A even more regularly than the day before. Olds next thought to see if the rat could be trained to visit a different corner. It only took five minutes. By giving it a small electric shock each time it took a step towards corner B, Olds got it there promptly. He wrote, 'After this the animal could be directed to almost any spot in the box at the will of the experimenter.'

The experiment was soon refined so that Olds did not have to push a button to get electricity to surge into the brain of the rat. That job was outsourced to the rat itself. The process is called intracranial self-stimulation and it involves putting a rat in a box with a lever that allows it to self-administer electric surges to the relevant parts of its brain.

There is ample video online of the rats in these experiments, and watching them is freaky. The wires that connect to the tops of their heads are thick and flexible, so the rats move around the cage freely. The terminus of these wires – the end where they are manipulated by the researchers – is out of sight. As you watch the rat hammer that lever your eye is drawn time and again to these wires. I found myself questioning the concept of free will, and thinking of old-fashioned gods, the kind who are never far offstage and intervene capriciously to shape individual destinies.

The apotheosis of this line of enquiry may have arrived in the 1960s when a researcher named Aryeh Routtenberg watched rats literally starve themselves to death in cages full of food.[2] The rats – all with electrodes implanted in their brains – would hammer the lever in their cages with ever-increasing intensity. Surge after surge of electricity would hit their brains. They would slow only as malnourishment caught up with them, and would finally stop – not to eat, but to expire. Is this torture? Did the rats die delirious with happiness? Would it be ethical even if that were the case? These questions are impossible to answer.

It was of course the neurotransmitter dopamine that was surging through these rats' brains, and it soon became clear that the dopamine reward centres of the brain are extremely powerful. Incentives activate these reward centres, triggering dopamine.

(This discovery that such powerful sensations of reward could be delivered to the brain remotely sparked a lot of science fiction.

The concept came to be known as wire-heading, which arguably represents a perverse incentive at the most meta level. If the goal of life is to do the things that make us happy, but we can short-circuit that, then we can meet the goal without taking any of the intended steps!)

The role of the brain in wanting and liking and learning is crucial to understanding incentives, as incentive systems exploit these neural pathways to change human behaviour. But research into the brain is new and progress has been slow. It's hard to look inside a brain and, despite advances in magnetic resonance imaging (MRI), which gives us a better idea of the workings of the brain, it's not always clear what scientists are seeing.

All this is to say that one reason the role of incentives in society is not fully appreciated is that the way the brain processes reward and punishment has not been established for long, and is still very much a work in progress.

But we do know some things. One of the things we know is that whether we are attracted to rewards or repulsed by punishments all depends on the operation of some very tiny molecules flitting around inside our brain.

Dopamine and company

It's important, before we go on, to learn a little about neurotransmitters. In the brain, as in great art, it is the spaces between that make all the difference. The brain is full of neurons – nerve cells. Between each neuron is a gap that must be crossed for messages to be sent. These gaps are called synapses and they're the source of all your happiness and sorrow.

Imagine a neuron reaching out to tap another neuron on the shoulder, then leaning in to whisper: 'I think we're happy.' That's one of the signals a neurotransmitter sends across a synapse. This is happening all the time, and in lots of synapses. Did I mention there are a lot of synapses? There are. In fact, the human brain contains over 100 trillion synapses.

I hate the word 'trillion'. Much like I hate the word 'billion'. Simply swapping a letter over at the start of the word does not do anything to convey the change in order of magnitude that we're experiencing. These words should make our jaws gape. (I wonder if this is why people appear so unfussed about wealth inequality in the anglosphere. Our language does very little to convey just how much bigger a billion is than a million.)

Here's a million:

Million.

Here's a billion:

Million million million million million million million million
million million million million million million million million
million million million million million million million million
million million million million million million million million
million million million million million million million million
million million million million million million million million
million million million million million million million million
million million million million million million million million
million million million million million million million million
million million million million million million million million
million million million million million million million million
million million million million million million million million
million million million million million million million million
million million million million million million million million
million million million million million million million million
million million million million million million million million
million million million million million million million million

million million million million million million million million
million million million million million million million million
million million million million million million million million
million million million million million million million million
million million million million million million million million
million million million million million million million million
million million million million million million million million
million million million million million million million million
million million million million million million million million
million million million million million million million million
million million million million million million million million
million million million million million million million million
million million million million million million million million
million million million million million million million million
million million million million million million million million
million million million million million million million million
million million million million million million million million
million million million million million million million million
million million million million million million million million
million million million million million million million million
million million million million million million million million
million million million million million million million million
million million million million million million million million
million million million million million million million million
million million million million million million million million
million million million million million million million million
million million million million million million million million
million million million million million million million million
million million million million million million million million
million million million million million million million million
million million million million million million million million
million million million million million million million million

million million million million million million million million
million million million million million million million million
million million million million million million million million
million million million million million million million million
million million million million million million million million
million million million million million million million million
million million million million million million million million
million million million million million million million million
million million million million million million million million
million million million million million million million million
million million million million million million million million
million million million million million million million million
million million million million million million million million
million million million million million million million million
million million million million million million million million
million million million million million million million million
million million million million million million million million
million million million million million million million million
million million million million million million million million
million million million million million million million million
million million million million million million million million
million million million million million million million million
million million million million million million million million
million million million million million million million million
million million million million million million million million
million million million million million million million million
million million million million million million million million
million million million million million million million million
million million million million million million million million
million million million million million million million million

million million million million million million million million
million million million million million million million million
million million million million million million million million
million million million million million million million million
million million million million million million million million
million million million million million million million million
million million million million million million million million
million million million million million million million million
million million million million million million million million
million million million million million million million million
million million million million million million million million
million million million million million million million million
million million million million million million million million
million million million million million million million million
million million million million million million million million
million million million million million million million million
million million million million million million million million
million million million million million million million million
million million million million million million million million
million million million million million million million million
million million million million million million million million
million million million million million million million million
million million million million million million million million
million million million million million million million million
million million million million million million million million
million million million million million million million million
million million million million million million million million
million million million million million million million million
million million million million million million million million
million million million million million million million million
million million million million million million million million
million million million million million million million million
million million million million million million million million

million million million million million million million million
million million million million million million million million
million million million million million million million million
million million million million million million million million
million million million million million million million million
million million million million million million million million
million million million million million million million million
million million million million million million million million
million million million million million million million million
million million million million million million million million
million million million million million million million million
million million million million million million million million
million million million million million million million million
million million million million million million million million
million million million million million million million million.

Let's waste no more paper repeating the point for trillions – suffice to say the scale of increase is the same.

The point of all the preceding material is to emphasise that the number of synapses we have is truly enormous. This is an immensely dense and complex system.

Messages travel across these countless synapses in the form of neurotransmitters. Thus neurotransmitters bridge the gaps between neurons. Some of these guys are famous – for example serotonin and oxytocin, often described as the 'love' hormones. Other powerful ones go incognito, like acetylcholine, which helps you wake up in the morning and keeps your memories in order (plus other things that science is still trying to figure out).

Among neurotransmitters, one in particular has crossed over to mainstream success and made itself a household name: dopamine. It's the most studied and best understood. Dopamine is, in the context of things, a small molecule: just 22 atoms glued together.

(Water by way of comparison is made of three atoms, while some of the proteins floating round in your body are made of hundreds and thousands. So dopamine is relatively small.) It's made of familiar stuff, like carbon, hydrogen, oxygen and nitrogen.

Dopamine is the hidden third character in this whole book. Whenever we talk about someone responding to an incentive, dopamine is there.

When you get a reward dopamine shoots out of neurons, flies across the gap to the other neuron, and hits a special spot called a receptor. The message is received – that you've had a reward. After a short time, the receptor lets the dopamine go and it returns to the original neuron so the message can be sent again later.

This is the basics of neurotransmitters: there are a lot of them, there are several different kinds, and they are very important to the processing of incentives.

Neurotransmitters are still a relatively recent discovery. The defining moment in the history of neurotransmitter research occurred in 1921. Until then, nobody believed neurons were shooting out little messengers. It was sacrilege to imagine that these cells, which pulsed with electricity, were sending out anything other than electricity. Two frogs had to die to end that notion.

A man named Otto Loewi, then a scientist in Vienna, took two frog hearts and designed an experiment that had come to him in a dream:

> *The night before Easter Sunday of that year I awoke, turned on the light, and jotted down a few notes on a tiny slip of thin paper. Then I fell asleep again. It occurred to me at six o'clock in the morning that during the night I had written down something most important, but I was unable to decipher the scrawl. The next night, at three o'clock, the idea returned. It was the design of an experiment to determine*

*whether or not the hypothesis of chemical transmission that I had
uttered seventeen years ago was correct. I got up immediately, went
to the laboratory, and performed a simple experiment on a frog heart
according to the nocturnal design.*[3]

Loewi put two frog hearts in two separate beakers of liquid. Each
was artificially made to beat. He made one heart beat faster, then he
moved liquid from that beaker to the other beaker. Lo and behold,
the second heart proceeded to beat faster too.

Nerves were not stimulated by electricity alone but also by tiny
particles – the theory that neurons emit neurotransmitters was proved!

(Actually it took many years, many arguments and a lot more
dead frogs before people believed Loewi. If this was a burden on
Loewi it was an even tougher era to be a frog, and we salute them for
their service to neuroscience.)

So neurotransmitters were known of for decades, but it was
much longer before science had any definitive ideas about how they
operate in the brain, where dopamine hosts its regular fireworks
displays. The science behind all this – and therefore on how and
why we respond to incentives – is terrifyingly new.

Fortunately, there have been thousands of experiments in recent
years showing the role of dopamine in incentive systems, on all
kinds of creatures. Scientists can get similar results from different
animals because dopamine neurons are what they call 'evolutionarily
conserved'. This means they show up in lots of different animals,
probably because they are so important to survival. After all, the
reward system exists to keep animals alive – it's what makes us pull
back from danger and push forward for a chance of food or water.
Incentives exploit these ancient systems.

Dopamine has been proven to make animals much more
sensitive to rewards. One wonderful experiment used mice that were

genetically wired to have hyperactive dopamine systems. They were brimming with dopamine, and it made them extremely sensitive to payoffs. The first thing the scientists did was show the mice Froot Loops, a brightly coloured breakfast cereal (the only arguable fruit content of which is some coconut oil in their partially hydrogenated vegetable oil component). The mice – high dopamine ones and 'wild type' controls – first needed to discover that the Froot Loops were tasty. That familiarisation went on for three days before the experiment began. Then, the mice were each placed in a box with sliding doors. Five grams of Froot Loops were placed in a second box, with the two boxes separated by a 'runway'. The scientists trained the mice to go along the runway and get the Froot Loops.

The high-dopamine mice performed very differently from the 'wild-type' mice. After a few training runs they went directly to the Froot Loops without changing direction in almost 80 per cent of cases. They sprinted without pausing in over 70 per cent of cases. The wild-type mice went directly in only 30 per cent of cases, and sprinted without pausing in only 20 per cent of cases. High-dopamine mice generally spent only four seconds getting distracted from their goal while for wild-type mice it was 12 seconds.

Scientists measured the mice's top running speeds, natural curiosity levels and even how much they liked Froot Loops to figure out if those were affecting the results. None of them were. If anything, the high-dopamine mice liked sugar slightly less and were more naturally curious, which should have given them less drive to go for the colourful little loops. But they didn't. The incentive operated especially strongly on the genetically altered mice because their brains were buzzing with dopamine.[4]

In a similar study scientists put rats in a cage with normal rat food available abundantly and special delicious rat pellets available by pressing a lever. The rats much preferred to eat the pellets and pressed the lever whenever they wished to eat. Then the scientists transformed the rats into low-dopamine animals by administering a drug that blocks a dopamine receptor. The rats gave up on pressing the lever and ate the rat food instead.[5]

Lessons from these studies may be applied – carefully – in the real world. Incentive designers must recognise that some people will be more like the high-dopamine mice, readily spurred to immediate and direct action by an incentive. Other people will not. Instead of thinking of non-responders as slow learners, consider thinking of them more charitably as low-dopaminers.

Liking and wanting

Another big breakthrough in recent neuroscience has been distinguishing between two different parts of the reward system – liking and wanting. Liking something and wanting it turn out to use different parts of the brain. One can be fired up without the other.

We know some aspects of this intuitively. For example, I like ice-cream but I don't want it right now. But there's a less intuitive aspect to the discovery: it's possible to 'want' things without liking them. For example, those with a drug dependency may want drugs even as they cognitively understand that they no longer enjoy taking them.

The difference between wanting and liking can be seen most clearly in a lab setting when scientists use a cue for introducing a reward. A cue is something that is introduced just prior to a reward to signal the reward is coming. For example: a foreign object introduced into a rat's cage just prior to a food pellet. (Scientists usually use a piece of metal as the foreign object.) The animals don't 'like' the cue but they come to want it. They often approach it, sniff it and some rats even chew it in advance of the food pellet arriving.[6]

It brings them no hedonic payoff (there is no liking) but the wanting parts of their brain are highly activated.

If you train a rat by showing it a cue when it's hungry, then later show it the cue when it's full, it will start eating. The cue itself helps drive the behaviour, not just the need for the reward. Cues can amplify wanting behaviours. This can be very handy to know when the reward is expensive (a cash prize) and the cue is cheap (a certificate or blue ribbon). We should be suspicious of our dopamine-driven desire to want the cue. A bit more cue and a bit less prize can probably motivate just as well as a big prize.

When we're on the receiving end of these 'cues', it's worth being highly suspicious. For example, poker machines that flash their lights intensely and play music for tiny payouts will get our dopamine systems running hot even as they steadily drain our wallets. If we recruit our cognitive centres to the question we can probably learn to avoid payoffs that are more about the cue than the reward.

Nature or nurture or incentives?

Look at the sun then look away: an after-effect remains in your vision for a while. Incentives are the same: their effects last not only because we respond to incentives, but also because we learn from them. Incentives can continue to have a powerful effect on our neurological reward system even after they've been removed.

What we tend to think of as inherent motivation or demotivation, morality or immorality, may be to some extent learned behaviour. We might learn to behave in a certain way – perhaps that lesson is about individuality, risk-taking, respect for authority or how much to trust strangers – and then have those lessons reinforced time and again by society. It will take powerful new incentives to reverse those learned behaviours.

You might even argue that a society's culture is just the behaviours generated by the incentives the society faces or faced, reinforced over time by social expectations. Cultures may remain long after the incentives that encouraged certain behaviours have dissipated. For example, Australians of European heritage often eat the foods of a northern hemisphere winter at Christmas, even though Christmas occurs in high summer in Australia. The incentives to gorge on potatoes and roast meats (i.e. cold weather and an absence of fresh vegetables) no longer apply, but they have been so well learned and so heavily reinforced by the set of incentives we call cultural expectations that they are now stuck.

Do you want to uproot behaviours that are reinforced by whole cultures? That will require extra-powerful incentives. When societies decide that culturally ingrained habits like drink driving are too risky, it requires dedication. Introducing rewards for changing behaviour and punishments for continuing old habits pits an incentive designer against a fearsome opponent indeed – dopamine pathways reinforced by learning. New incentives may be very slow to make progress. The upside is that when an incentive designer can *create* a new culture – a set of behaviours that are reinforced by other people's behaviour – they can expect it to endure.

Interlude

A Mannish Jape

In 2013, I began to develop a sharp pain in my abdomen. The cause was two pieces of metal: a hook and eye, designed to fasten a pair of trousers.

Their attack on me could be seen as an entirely justified protest at how I was straining their capacities. Those metal pieces were coming under pressure from three directions – pulled left and right with intensifying force, and also under attack from directly behind, as an increasingly heavy man bore down on them.

To be clear, my suit trousers no longer fit. I had grown fat.

As the year went on, I got even fatter. I had a desk job and each afternoon, slumped in my swivel chair, I would empty a packet of peanut M&Ms (kilojoules: 984) onto my desk and sort them into colours. I then proceeded to gobble them like a parody of a stressed and unhealthy salaried worker.

On a few especially shameful occasions I bought a packet of Tim Tams (kilojoules: 4320), stowed it in my desk drawer, and emptied it within a few hours.

Swivelling in my swivel chair and mousing with my mouse was, shockingly, not enough exercise to counter all the chocolatey sweets.

Repetition of this routine had the result of moving the needle on my scales in a clockwise direction until it finally pointed at a whopping (for me at the time*) 80 kilograms. I began wearing jeans to work because my suit was at bursting point.

I wobbled through the winter. The newspaper bureau at which

----

* I now weigh more than that again. But this time a fair bit of the weight is muscle. I think. Probably. Look, just ignore this footnote.

I worked was immediately across the road from a supermarket that had just opened and was selling a lot of snack food at very low prices. (Those packs of Tim Tams? Often only a dollar. One Australian dollar! How could you not?) I made regular missions across the road to see what they had on special.

One day, coming back from the supermarket with my snacks, I saw recently deposed Australian prime minister Kevin Rudd emerge from the newspaper building, pursued by journalists from other publications. None of my colleagues were there, and I real-ised I should probably keep an eye on him in case he was about to make any comments. Sure enough Mr Rudd – never exactly media shy – stopped on the roadside and gave a quick doorstop press conference. I waddled along and began to record what he was saying.

A photographer was apparently at this impromptu event because a picture was later widely disseminated. It shows a man with a grey plastic supermarket bag in one hand (that's me) holding a micro-phone beneath the eminent politician's nose. I'm in profile and there is something incongruous about the image, I admit. Few expect a journalist to interview an ex-PM on the way back from the shops.

I showed it to a mate, expecting a comment on my initiative. 'You look fat,' they said.

Around November I left the newspaper, but the habits of the swivel chair were hard to break. The year crawled to a slovenly and piggish conclusion, but eventually, sickened and sorry about what I had become, I made a pledge: I would lose the weight.

I planned to shed 4 kilograms in a month, beginning as the new year dawned. On 1 January 2014, I declined to sate my fuzzy head-ache with fatty foods or soft drink and instead drank a lot of water. My month of moderation began.

The 31 days of January stretched out in front of me like a Sahara of self-denial. But I did not fear failing in my journey through these arid lands. The driving force that kept me plodding onward was a promise that I made publicly.

'I pledge to pay $500 in penalties if the 4 kg is not lost by the morning of February 1,' I wrote on my blog.

Just to ramp up the suspense, the donation I give if I fail will be to the Motoring Enthusiasts Party … The Motoring Enthusiasts could not be further from my affections. The thought of a slice of my recent redundancy payment going to them will be a strong motivator in case anyone opens a Haigh's Dessert Block in front of me during January. The Motoring Enthusiasts will not see a cent. This is my pledge.

For anyone unfamiliar with Australian chocolate and politics, allow me to introduce both the Haigh's Dessert Block and the Motoring Enthusiasts Party. The former is a delicious high-end confection suspended halfway between milk chocolate and dark, while the latter was an upstart political party that entered the Australian political scene in 2013 with a policy platform that advocated for the freedom to make car modifications.

(Interestingly, the Motoring Enthusiasts Party's sole parliamentary representative soon came to realise the job of being a federal senator is about far more than drilling out a few mufflers. He eventually became something of a voice of reason in that parliament. Had I foreseen this agreeable outcome, god only knows how sumo-esque I would be by now.)

The public incentive – plus regular weigh-ins that I posted to my blog – were meant to keep me on the straight and narrow.

I began to start the day with black coffee instead of white. I counted out meagre rations of almonds instead of stuffing great handfuls of them in my mouth. I weighed serves of yoghurt and read the calorie content on all manner of packets. When you start to do this, you learn a lot.

I learned that what looks like a small serve of something might not be. For example, nuts pack a lot of energy into a tiny volume. I learned that fat earned its bad reputation by being amazingly high in calories. Amazingly. I also learned that the recommended daily caloric intake was far less than what I had been eating.

I wrote down everything I ate in the notes app in my phone. Here's the fifth day of the diet:

Muesli: 1000 kJ.

Coffee: 200 kJ.

Nectarine: 80 kJ.

Sandwich: 1500 kJ.

Nuts: 700 kJ.

Cordial: 400 kJ.

Chicken cacciatore: 3000 kJ.

Total: 7000 kJ.

That was a representative day for food. There were some where I ate less and some where I came in a little higher.

The scales reacted pretty quickly. I'm not sure why but the weight seems to come off quickly when you first restrict your eating. Is that water weight? Stuff, ahem, in transit? Whatever it is, you can make a 2-kilo difference within the first week.

After that it got hard. Sometimes I had a headache in the afternoon and my productivity would plummet. But I learned to live with the feeling of hunger, and just accept it was a thing that would be there. (This was 2014, mind you, before anyone had even heard of mindfulness. So yeah, it's possible I invented that, but no sweat to all the yoga teachers out there, I'm not going to come round pressing copyright claims. You're welcome.)

Eventually, though, the pain paid off. Changes became visible not only on the scale but in the mirror. The suggestion of ribs became a clear statement: RIBS. What I'd always considered to be well-built pectoral muscles stopped jiggling so much. The tyre around the middle went from a mountain bike tyre to a hybrid commuter bike tyre.

In fact, I reached the target weight with over a week to spare and ended up coming in under the goal. The huge threat of failure hovering over me – combined with daily updates – meant friends and acquaintances were engaged with the whole process.

It was still hard and lonely and I got very hungry. But the social aspect meant there was one sense in which it was fun.

A postscript to the whole experience came after pitching a story about my weight loss to *The Guardian*. They agreed to run it online, which pleased me. Trouble began when they gave it the following headline: 'How I lost weight by pledging to give money to a political party I loathe.'

The comments section went berserk. People did not like my cunning plan. They thought my weight-loss plan a scam.

'You could find no better motivator than your hatred of other people enjoying their hobby? This is truly sad, I think you may have issue[s],' wrote one person.[1]

The reaction got under my skin. I had never expressed hatred for the Motoring Enthusiasts Party at all. I very deliberately chose my language and it never included an expression of hatred. 'They could not be further from my affections,' I wrote, and 'The prospect of sending cash to them makes me shiver.' A *Guardian* subeditor chucked the word 'loathe' into the headline (probably because those deliberate circumlocutions were hard to summarise).

So it wasn't me saying 'hate'! It was the subeditor! I could rant and rave all I wanted, but by that point the comments section was 100 deep and the point of changing it was gone.

Incidentally, that separation between journalists and subeditors over who authorises headlines is the source of a huge number of misleading headlines. So why hasn't the problem been fixed? After all, it could be – subeditors no longer need to have authorship of headlines to make them fit awkward spots in the newspaper layout. Here's one theory: it's an awfully convenient separation. It lends plausible deniability to journos who know at some subterranean level that sometimes the most effective headline gently obscures the story's content. The incentive structures here are bad.

We return now to the *Guardian* commenters who are still letting loose on me: 'How can you "loathe" a political party that neither you nor anyone else knows anything about? Or are you just another hysterical hyper-exaggerator who only has extreme emotional reactions to the blandest of topics?' asked one commenter, apparently without irony.

But the very best response came from a commenter under the name Malasangra, who utterly confounded my entire plan. That person wrote the following comment, (transcribed verbatim): 'I pledge to give $2,000 to the Australian Motoring Enthusiasts Party if Jason Murphy looses weight this month.'

One can't know if the person ever followed through – I hope not – but it was a brilliant and inspired attempt to confound me through the use of incentives. I felt a great kinship. Is that how Batman feels about the Joker? I'm not sure. But I still smile when I imagine Malasangra typing that out.

A final enduring souvenir from the comment section was the person who described my endeavours as 'a mannish jape'. That turn of phrase appealed deeply to my beloved, and has became a catch-cry of hers whenever I embark on an endeavour she considers a touch silly.

Part 2

Incentives in Action

Chapter 6

Less Than a Loaf of Bread

In Part 2 we travel deep inside the beating hearts of several major incentive systems. We will start with an incentive system that beats very loud indeed: the price system. Prices, we will see, are not just a minor numerical feature of going to the shops but a major incentive system governing our lives.

The year was 2011 and I was living on the fringes of the inner city, in the hipster ghetto. The most remarkable feature of the neighbourhood was the quality of the sourdough. My tastebuds weep just to recall it.

The finest purveyor of sourdough in that region was a bakery called Dench. The hipsters would come from miles around. First thing in the hipster morning (which is to say around 10.30 am) the streets were full of people riding home from Dench with a loaf balanced on the handlebars of their vintage steel bikes.

But Dench made you pay for it. Walking out of Dench Bakers with a crusty sourdough you would find yourself A$8.20 poorer. Compared to $3.50 for a perfectly acceptable loaf of multigrain from the supermarket across the street, it was a hard choice. I lusted after the fancy sourdough. And yet I am frugal. I did not want to waste money.

The choice between the good bread and the cheap was one I weighed often, and so it happened that over time, little by little, I became attuned to the price of bread. How, I found myself wondering, did it get so high? All that pondering gave me the opportunity one day to have my mind blown. Someone told me the price of toasters at Woolworths supermarket.

They cost ... wait for it ... for a totally real, perfectly normal, Australian Standards–complying, two-slice unit ... a scarcely believable $7.99. Which was, I remind you, less than the price of a loaf of Dench sourdough. A toaster costing less than a loaf of bread? This engineered contrivance of heavy steel, intricate copper and highly refined petrochemicals, combined thousands of miles away in an unimaginable foreign factory – could it cost less than a simple blend of flour and water?

I swayed under the heavy weight of this new and scarcely believable fact.

Now, I was not unaware that these were the extremes of both categories. Plenty of people across Australia were still paying $1 for a supermarket loaf of bread. Meanwhile, others were buying the Magimix Vision toaster for $499. (It has glass walls so you can see your toast browning.) I do not pretend for a moment that the Venn diagram of the prices of toasters and loaves has any more than a sliver of intersection. But still. Inside me burned a fierce, stubborn flame that said the two circles ought never to meet.

Yet meet they did.

In Sydney, a still more exclusive bakery called Sonoma was selling loaves of sourdough for $14. Or, as I like to think of it, almost two whole toasters per loaf.

I was working as a financial journalist at the time, and so I wrote a short piece about the economics of this situation. I researched the amazing inflation in bread (which tends to go stale on a slow boat, so has to be made domestically) and contrasted it with the anaemic price rises in small household domestic appliances (straight out of south-east China.)

I interviewed the guy who kept the books at my local bakery. 'Wages have gone up a lot,' the Dench operations manager told me. 'Bread is predominantly flour and water and that isn't really the cost, it's the cost of getting that flour to us and the cost of paying humans to mould it.'[1]

The reason Dench sourdough was expensive was complex – a mix of local wages and transport. The reason toasters were cheap was also complex – to do with Chinese wages and transport. The story hit a nerve and people talked about it a lot.

Prices are something people care about. People love to boast about getting a bargain and, paradoxically, also love to subtly let people know how expensive their possessions are.

Economists put prices at the centre of the study of how the world works. But the way they work on *people* is often glossed over. I had been thinking about prices and incentives and bread and toasters for a long time before I fully grasped that prices are not just incentives but a complete incentive system. A vast and extremely powerful one.

Our constant companions

Prices were a feature of human society from the beginning. When archaeologists uncover the earliest pieces of writing, they usually turn out to be invoices. One notable such piece is from 5000 BC, from ancient Mesopotamia – a receipt for clothing written in cuneiform script pressed into clay.

The co-evolution of prices and civilisation is, some say, not a coincidence. One philosopher says we 'stumbled upon' the system of prices 'without understanding it'. That was the famous economist Friedrich Hayek. He argues it was very lucky because it allowed humans to best organise our societies and economies – that is, that prices allowed civilisation to develop.

Doesn't he have the causation back to front? Doesn't civilisation cause prices, not the other way round? Hayek says no:

> *The people who like to deride any suggestion that this may be so usually distort the argument by insinuating that it asserts that by some miracle just that sort of system has spontaneously grown up which is best suited to modern civilization. It is the other way round: man has been able to develop that division of labor on which our civilization is based because he happened to stumble upon a method which made it possible.*[2]

This is a big claim. But it's one I agree with.

Hayek argues two things: that humans didn't invent the price system on purpose, and that the blossoming of our civilisations depends on prices. That we are the beneficiaries of a happy accident.

It's entirely true that prices actually predate money. A price really just expresses the value of one thing in terms of something else. Even bartering required prices of a sort: one sheep for a pair of shoes, etc.

People bartered for all sorts of goods – from milk and bread that would only last a day, to long-lasting items like tools and raw materials. Bartering for long-lasting goods was probably a precursor to money – if it would last it could be saved and used to barter again later. But the invention of currency was like pouring petrol on the fire for the price incentive. Money, if you think about it, is just an IOU for a future barter with persons unknown. This is a huge step up.

Prices expressed in terms of money give us enormous freedom to trade with a much wider set of people. They allow us to trade more and trade better. Ultimately they allow us to stop being generalists and become specialists. The reason specialised jobs exist, like apple farmer, smiths and tailors, is that prices allow us to trade efficiently. We don't have to grow our own apples, forge our own iron and sew our own clothes. And that makes life better. When we specialise, we can improve our work. When we trade what we make, everyone benefits from that improvement.

In part, cities grew up because the more customers you can find the more you can trade and the more you can specialise. The flipside is that living in cities gave you access to a bigger range of goods made by more specialised artisans. Prices coordinated that process. This is what Hayek was describing. The price system helped create our modern world, our civilisation.

Incentives and prices clearly have a lot in common. For a seller the system is simple: give up your item and get a monetary reward. If that monetary reward is high enough the seller will work to make the item in large quantities (or grow it, import it, etc.). They will also work to make that item cheaply.

For the buyer the incentive is just the reverse. Give up the money, get the good. So far, so obvious.

The interesting part is that the incentive can work in both directions at once – both buyer and seller are incentivised by the same price. That is because the buyer and seller put different subjective values on the good. For the seller the good is worth less than the price and for the buyer the good is worth more than the price. These differences in how people subjectively value goods are necessary for trade. If everyone put the same subjective value on everything, nothing would ever change hands!

Prices work simultaneously as incentives on buyers and sellers.

It prods both buyers and sellers in the same direction – to make a trade. If they aren't selling enough, sellers will work to make prices lower. If they can't buy enough, buyers will work to get more money. This double effect of prices is an especially serendipitous feature of an accidental incentive system. Not all incentives work on multiple parties at once and encourage them to cooperate.

The other reason the price incentive is so powerful is that it doesn't require central coordination. Which is not to say that we don't regulate some prices – nor is it to say we shouldn't. But a price system can be relied on to spring into existence almost anywhere and to self-regulate. These features are extremely impressive and very surprising. But they don't mean the price system is magical or above reproach. In fact, this very powerful system generates some powerful side effects.

Side effects

Just as the rat-tail bounty we looked at in Part 1 made people hunt rats, so the world of prices makes people hunt money. Some people hunt money fair and square, and we call them business owners. Some people try to hand in mouse and vole tails to get their reward – we call them counterfeiters. Still other people try to farm money, just as the Vietnamese farmed rats. We call them investors.

The parallel breaks down a bit here because, unlike the Vietnamese rat farmers, investors do not totally undermine the intent of the price system. Instead they partly help reinforce it and, in part, provide the money businesses need to grow. This helps the whole economy tick along. This is what Friedrich Hayek was talking about when he said the price system helped create civilisation. It not only encourages beneficial trades; some of its side effects are beneficial as well.

The price system evolved naturally, and it tends to resist being controlled: when governments have tried to do away with a decentralised price system things tend to get messy rather swiftly. From the Soviets to the Venezuelans, it has become clear that a society cannot control prices for everything. (Which is not to say it shouldn't control prices for some things.)

Prices did not get much academic attention for a very long time, perhaps because they seemed so natural they were hard to notice. Economics as a discipline did not emerge until thousands of years later than history, medicine or natural sciences (which is arguably why it remains so underdeveloped). The first person to really think about prices was Adam Smith. Sadly, he got it mostly wrong.

Adam Smith lived between 1723 and 1790, and was a member of the Scottish Enlightenment as well as becoming the most famous early economist. He had a few ideas about prices; namely, he believed they should be related to input costs.

Smith believed that things had a 'natural price':

When the price of any commodity is neither more nor less than what is sufficient to pay the rent of the land, the wages of the labour, and the profits of the stock employed in raising, preparing, and bringing it to market, according to their natural rates, the commodity is then sold for what may be called its natural price.[3]

This is a logical conclusion and it applies in some circumstances. But he missed the most important concepts in all of economics: supply and demand. And little more insight was gained into the nature of prices until much later, in the twentieth century.

The best and most famous analysis of prices was published by Hayek in 1945. Even though it's very good, I'm nervous about citing it. Hayek has a reputation. He has ardent fans from a narrow section of society and is known as being a particularly ideological economist, based on a lot of things he wrote that are not about prices.

Much of Hayek's work is vehemently anti-government. (In a moment we'll see why. Hayek could see all the ways in which an accidentally developed incentive scheme could work. He believed passionately in decentralised systems that operate without a controlling entity. He was hopelessly in love with the free market. But Hayek could not or would not see the many ways in which such a decentralised system could fail.)

The wonderful economic historian J Bradford DeLong reckons he sees three Hayeks:

1. *The (absolutely brilliant) price-system-as-information-aggregator Hayek.*
2. *the (absolutely bonkers) business-cycle 'liquidationist' Hayek.*
3. *the (absolutely wrong) social-democracy-is-evil Hayek.*

The first was a genius. The second was a moron — he could never make his arguments cohere either conceptually or empirically, but he kept doubling down on them and wound up in infinite reputational bankruptcy. The third was wrong — I would say blinded ex ante by ideology, others would say proved wrong ex post by events. The problem is that the modern-day Hayekians are by-and-large uninterested in the good Hayek (1), and interested only in the bad Hayeks (2) and (3) ...[4]

Continuing this tradition, we will be using a scalpel to carve out the 'genius' parts of the good Hayek and show why the wrong and bonkers elements are wrong and bonkers. Both aspects are illustrative of incentives.

Hayek's great idea was to see how prices were made. They represented a summary of information. That information came from far and wide. If a storm ripped through the banana fields of Queensland, the price of bananas went up, reflecting that information. It didn't overload the buyer with detail about maximum gusts or the number of banana palms destroyed. It just summarised all that info into a higher price.

Hayek makes the same point in this next excerpt. Being from Austria and born in the nineteenth century, rather than Australia in the twentieth, he chooses tin as his example, not bananas.

> *Assume that somewhere in the world a new opportunity for the use of some raw material, say, tin, has arisen, or that one of the sources of supply of tin has been eliminated. It does not matter for our purpose – and it is very significant that it does not matter – which of these two causes has made tin more scarce. All that the users of tin need to know is that some of the tin they used to consume is now more profitably employed elsewhere and that, in consequence, they must economize tin. There is no need for the great majority of them even to know where the more urgent need has arisen, or in favor of what other needs they ought to husband the supply.*[5]

Higher prices of bananas or tin bring the quantity demanded down until the amount of bananas or tin that people wanted to buy was roughly equal to the amount that were available for sale. Prices vary according to the amount supplied.

Hayek is, quite rightly, impressed with the way prices coordinate the amount of things traded, so that the amount people can afford to buy equals out to the amount that sellers have been able to provide.

Earlier I said Hayek's analysis was very good. And it is. But there is a great deal missing from his famous essay on prices as information. What about supply, Friedrich? What about supply?

In his discussion of tin Hayek fails to mention how the rising price should have an equally significant effect on suppliers of tin, and *potential* suppliers of tin. If they can get tin out of storage or source some from somewhere, now would be a great time to do so. Prices don't just make people conserve tin, they make people provide it. They act as an incentive on both sides of the market.

We can see in the next passage just how enthused he is on just the demand side. One can only imagine how ebullient he would have been had he seen that the effect has *two* sides.

> *The marvel is that in a case like that of a scarcity of one raw material, without an order being issued, without more than perhaps a handful of people knowing the cause, tens of thousands of people whose identity could not be ascertained by months of investigation, are made to use the material or its products more sparingly; i.e. they move in the right direction ... I am convinced that if it were the result of deliberate human design, and if the people guided by the price changes understood that their decisions have significance far beyond their immediate aim, this mechanism would have been acclaimed as one of the greatest triumphs of the human mind. Its misfortune is the double one that it is not the product of human design and that the people guided by it usually do not know why they are made to do what they do.*[6]

Hayek's love for prices is pure and super endearing. But the next section of the essay starts to gives us some clues as to why he had his peculiar blind spots.

> *[T]hose who clamor for conscious direction ... should remember this: The problem is precisely how to extend the span of our utilization of resources beyond the span of the control of any one mind; and therefore, how to dispense with the need of conscious control, and how to provide inducements which will make the individuals do the desirable things without anyone having to tell them what to do.*[7]

Hayek is saying we should put our faith in the price system and not ask a society to tell its members what to do. This aversion is very important to understanding Hayek: he is rebutting calls for centrally planned economies. Hayek published all the above quotes in 1945, in a paper called 'The Use of Knowledge in Society'. If he obsesses on how a market channels information, it is because his intellectual enemies were arguing that central planning would be superior at processing information. Hayek places his faith in a decentralised system and in many markets he is right: prices do a better job than centralised planning.

But Hayek took his commitment to a decentralised price system a lot further and argued almost any government planning leads to tyranny. He opposed powerful governments of all kinds and went, frankly, much too far.

The era in which Hayek wrote explains a lot. Fascism was in ascendance during his most intellectually fertile periods. Writing during the Second World War an Austrian-born person might quite justifiably be suspicious of centralised authority and strong governments. But of course the British Government that sheltered Hayek during the war was also pretty centralised (rationing, anyone?) and it managed to end up on the side of freedom. Power can be used for good as well as evil.

The ability to set and enforce large, centralised incentive schemes is of course a form of power, and not all centralised power is used fairly. Hayek believed it never could be. But that is too pessimistic an outlook. Government can be an instrument for collective action rather than an evil overlord. Indeed it is collective action we need to get us out of some of the traps created by accidental and perverse incentives. We need laws and rules and systems to help steer us around those traps, and government is proven to be a decent way of steering.

As a corollary to his suspicion of power, Hayek wrote eloquently in defence of the importance of the little guy:

Today it is almost heresy to suggest that scientific knowledge is not the sum of all knowledge ... [yet] practically every individual has some advantage over all others because he possesses unique information of which beneficial use might be made.[8]

Hayek was making the point that the diverse participants in an economy have information that lets the price incentive work. It's a really good insight and one that can be extended beyond prices. We'll see something similar in a later chapter, on irrigation, that is not organised via a free market. Dispersed information can be harnessed by incentive schemes – even incentive schemes that are not prices – and that makes Hayek's insight more powerful, not less.

So Hayek was onto something. The reason the price system works so brilliantly as an incentive system is it is continually tweaked by the little people on the ground. It turns out that constant tweaking is essential for an incentive system, as we shall soon see.

Merchants adapt prices all the time. How high a price is too high? The answer changes constantly. Hayek believes the constant price changes by millions of individual sellers do the coordinating so the rest of us can relax and not worry about how the price system operates.

Hayek liked to quote another philosopher, called Alfred Whitehead. Whitehead famously argued against mindfulness:

It is a profoundly erroneous truism, repeated by all copy-books and by eminent people when they are making speeches, that we should cultivate the habit of thinking what we are doing. The precise opposite is the case. Civilization advances by extending the number of important operations which we can perform without thinking about them.[9]

This is a neat aphorism. Of course we all use things without worrying about how they work. The espresso machine on my kitchen bench is an occult mystery to me, the electronic devices in my home more so. But while not thinking about incentives is all well and good for the average Joe being led by prices to buy a certain kind of coffee bean, no price system – nor any incentive system – works perfectly without anyone thinking about it or overseeing it.

Even the best incentives need oversight, because all incentive systems can create accidental incentives, can be exploited, and can begin to decay. If we let the economy run along wholly on its own, then sure, it may surprise us with its productive capacity. But soon enough we could find ourselves in a different kind of hell. More pollution. Low-quality products. Poverty. The economic system is good at matching supply and demand and cares little what sort of mess it makes in the process.

Of course, libertarians and free marketeers often want the economy to tick along unmolested. They cite Hayek and they also refer to Adam Smith, whose 'invisible hand' is a trope that is often used to argue that the economy looks after itself best without supervision. You've probably heard of the invisible hand many times before. But what you haven't seen, perhaps, is where this term comes from. Here's the source of the quote:

> *By preferring the support of domestic to that of foreign industry, he intends only his own security; and by directing that industry in such a manner as its produce may be of the greatest value, he intends only his own gain, and he is in this, as in many other cases, led by an invisible hand to promote an end which was no part of his intention. Nor is it always the worse for the society that it was not part of it. By pursuing his own interest he frequently promotes that of the society more effectually than when he really intends to promote it. I have*

never known much good done by those who affected to trade for the public good. It is an affectation, indeed, not very common among merchants, and very few words need be employed in dissuading them from it.[10] [Emphasis mine.]

This quote is often presented without the first clause, 'By preferring the support of domestic to that of foreign industry'. When that is included it becomes clear Smith is not in fact arguing for free enterprise, or even totally free trade between nations without taxes or tariffs. He is arguing for people investing in their own countries even if they could make more money investing abroad. In a sense he is arguing against being guided by market forces.

Smith has another very famous quote that actually better makes the point people imagine they are making when they cite the invisible hand. It argues that price incentives are a terrific way of organising society, and it is presented below in context.

*In almost every other race of animals each individual, when it is grown up to maturity, is entirely independent, and in its natural state has occasion for the assistance of no other living creature. But man has almost constant occasion for the help of his brethren, and it is in vain for him to expect it from their benevolence only. He will be more likely to prevail if he can interest their self-love in his favour, and show them that it is for their own advantage to do for him what he requires of them. Whoever offers to another a bargain of any kind, proposes to do this. Give me that which I want, and you shall have this which you want, is the meaning of every such offer; and it is in this manner that we obtain from one another the far greater part of those good offices which we stand in need of. **It is not from the benevolence of the butcher, the brewer, or the baker that we expect our dinner, but from their regard to their own interest.***

We address ourselves, not to their humanity but to their self-love, and never talk to them of our own necessities but of their advantages.[11]
[Emphasis mine.]

Now, I like this quote a lot. It is one of the core tenets of economics, and its insight fires the ideas in this book. If you can provide the right incentives, you can get desirable behaviour from anyone, benevolent or otherwise. The economic system provides some of the right incentives.

But this book also argues against taking that insight too far. Just because the butcher, baker and brewer's self-interest keep the Smith family fed doesn't mean we should let them run amok. Economic self-interest could cause a brewer to water down beer, a baker to underpay staff, or a butcher to dispose of waste in the river. Self-interest serves the common interest best when we supervise and corral it to make sure one person's interest is not pitted against the rest.

What's more, the need to guide the behaviour of business grows as business grows. Smith wrote 250 years ago, when most businesses were small artisans, and many governments were large and dangerous empires. (The Dutch and British East India companies are excluded from the ranks of small artisans here. Smith, to his credit, was a critic of their rapacious, monopolistic business model. Note that when he speaks of the charms of the price system, he sings the praises of the little guys.) These days, several large multinational businesses are stronger than all but a few governments. (If you're reading this book in China, you may scoff at the idea that business is more powerful than government. For the rest of us, it's increasingly true.) The alchemy of the price incentive system may turn a small baker's self-interest into a force for good, but the self-interest of a major multinational is a rather more stubborn substance.

Prices are a powerful way to arrange the world, and to some degree they function without regulation, but that does not mean we just sit back and let business ride. Some of the ways businesses work to reduce prices are brilliant. They efficiently discover a new battery chemistry that means phones can be cheaper, for example. Other ways to cut prices come with downsides. Some businesses will underpay staff or fail to invest in safe working conditions. They also strive to win market power so that they can set prices without regard to competition and devour tasty profits.

Incentives hit some people, some of the time

Incentives function stochastically, which is just a fancy way of saying we don't know who they'll affect but we know they'll affect someone. Put another way, they don't work on every individual, but behave predictably in aggregate.

Each person or business feels free, but the weight of the incentives is pulling relentlessly on their choice. Even the sternest incentive won't operate on everybody. Capital punishment has not eradicated the worst crimes in the places where it operates. Conversely, even the weakest incentive may spur a few people. In the business context, this means that given a chance to raise profits a few percentage points by cutting wages below legal levels, a tiny share of businesses will.

The effect of incentive schemes matters more as the world grows larger and more complex. If a system entices one person in a thousand to misbehave, that might not be a problem of any relevance at first. But as the world grows ever more populous, even small accidental, perverse or missing incentives can create problems of genuine magnitude and social importance. Economists often call these side effects 'externalities' and they include, for just one example, the emission of carbon dioxide into the atmosphere in a way that scientists overwhelmingly believe is causing the globe to heat up.

A growing economy is extremely good for human well-being – living standards are rising as more people can afford food, clean water, electricity, education and sanitation. As our economy grows, the more we can see the failures of incentives mounting, and the more they also come to affect our living standards. It's increasingly important to identify and deal with them.

Chapter 7

Crazy Bargains (and Crazy Luxury)

In our house we eat a lot of rice crackers. These are small, circular crackers that come in a packet that says on the outside 'Baked not Fried'. I have no delusions about what rice crackers are – potato chips for people who imagine themselves too healthy or sophisticated to eat potato chips. Precisely how rice crackers squeezed out such a niche in our lives and on our supermarket shelves is unclear, but it doesn't matter so much. They're still delivering salty carbs, and with the bonus of letting us feel we're making mindful food choices.

When I look at rice crackers on the supermarket shelf, at A$0.90 per pack, I can't help but buy them. What's most amazing about these extremely inexpensive snacks is that they come from the other side of the world. They're made in China. This is why people worry about food miles, I guess. It seems crazy and wasteful that food comes from so far away when we can grow it or make it right here.

I understand that perspective. But I suspect many of the people who worry about food miles have no idea the strength of the forces domestic food production is up against. Shipping these days ain't what it used to be … It's fiercely, violently, desperately efficient.

400 metres long and a crew of 13

Shipping containers are an amazing invention. They make moving things easy. The modern intermodal shipping container was first used in 1955, and resulted in a drastic reduction in shipping costs. One measure of the price of shipping is the Baltic Dry Index. A glance at the index is enough to make a person breathe a deep sigh of relief that they're not a mariner. Prices have been tumbling for years.[1] As they do, the shipping industry is moving increasing volumes. In 2000, 225 million 20-foot-equivalent containers went through the world ports. In 2017, the number of shipping containers moved was more than three times higher.[2]

Shipping grows more popular as it gets cheaper. Let's go back to our bargain rice crackers and figure out the component of their cost that is due to shipping.

The price of shipping a container from Shanghai to Australia is low. It varies but is at times under US$500. That's for a TEU (20-foot equivalent unit), which has around 30 cubic metres of space in it. A ship can carry 20,000 such containers, which provides for revenue of up to $10 million a voyage.

Assume you can fit 10,000 packets of rice crackers in a 20-foot container. And factor in another US$500 for landing costs (grocery wholesalers are buying stevedoring services in bulk, remember). That's $1000 in shipping costs you must spread over 10,000 packets of crackers. That's just ten cents each, and when it's so low it doesn't matter much if it's US cents or Australian cents. No wonder they can sell them for $0.90 per packet. With goods that are more expensive and smaller – jars of olives, say – the cost of importation is even less important in relative terms.

Shipping is a great example of how a seemingly small price incentive can slowly but surely reshape the world. Why are there so few manufacturing jobs left in the US? Because shipping is so cheap. Moving jobs to China makes business sense. Savings on manufacture need be only a few cents per item to justify moving a whole factory. Why is there no longer an automotive industry in Australia? Because shipping is so cheap. The shipping cost advantages of making cars here are so slight they cannot possibly overcome the cost advantages of building in Thailand (where one quarter of Australia's cars are built, using labour paid around A$550 a month).

The low cost of shipping would be irrelevant if all other input costs were equal around the world. But the advent of cheap shipping has made it worthwhile to hunt out places with low input cost and make things there. Toasters are cheaper than bread for this reason – not only is shipping toasters cheap, but making them in China is too.

I'd argue the global politics of the last 20 years – the rise of China, and the equal but opposite rise of Donald Trump (a self-declared 'tariff man') – can be explained by industrial changes wrought in part by the falling cost of shipping. A price incentive is an enormously powerful force. When prices change, the world changes.

There are some excellent mechanical engineering reasons for why shipping is cheaper now. Containers can take a lot of the credit, and I don't wish to deny the importance of physical changes. But I do wish to direct our attention to the way they change incentives. The brilliant engineering partly explains these changed incentives, and these incentives ripple outward through the world in ways those engineers never imagined.

Like the French sewer system we looked at in Part 1, container-ised shipping is a rational, modern and optimised approach, in this case applied to the movement of goods. Like a sewer, global trade is a big system connecting all of us. And just as the French sewer system did, shipping has multiple outcomes. It operates in the way we want, and it also acts as a vector for side effects we didn't necessarily expect – not only large volumes of ships belching pollution into the atmosphere (the diesel they use is the world's dirtiest, and one claim is that when it comes to sulphurous emissions, the 16 biggest ships emit as much as all the world's cars[3]), but also major industrial change and even global political change.

There's another aspect of shipping we should look at, because it provides a very neat lesson on ways in which price incentives can be destructive. The price of shipping is affected by the location the ships are registered in. Ship owners love to choose 'flags of convenience', which is just a jaunty nautical term for talking about tax minimisation.

Many, many ships are registered in Panama, where the taxes are a fraction of what they would be in the US or Australia and the marine regulations are easy.[4] (Flags of convenience also help ship-owners avoid other laws – the very first foreign ships on the Panamanian register were US ships registered during prohibition and stocked to the gunwales with booze.) This is a problem for other nations that would like to collect taxes on the shipping businesses; highly mobile businesses like shipping can move to wherever in the world they like.

Later in this book we'll look at how incentives behave like they are evolving. Fit ones thrive and weak ones drop out. But fitness – what makes an incentive survive and expand and sometimes replicate – is not always the same as usefulness to humans.

Low taxes on business can be described as an evolutionarily fit incentive system. If one jurisdiction cuts taxes, businesses go there. Other jurisdictions feel they are obliged to compete. One term that has been used to describe this is 'a race to the bottom'. Such a race can be helpful when taxes are too high – but only up to a point. Lower taxes are not always a good idea. Governments need revenue to operate.

Regardless of taxes, Panama is a convenient place to register a ship since a lot of ships will be passing through there on their way from the Atlantic to the Pacific Ocean via the Panama Canal.

The Panama Canal is itself an interesting story about the power of incentives. It was of course built as a way to reduce the cost of shipping. The French started building it in the late nineteenth century. The building of the Suez Canal in Egypt just a few decades earlier had been a French triumph, but in Panama things were different. Their workforce was exhausted (tens of thousands died, largely due to dysentery and malaria) and their money ran out (angry investors lost hundreds of millions of dollars). Eventually the Americans took over.

The Panama Canal's construction should not be underestimated. It's very wide and very long and it goes through some rugged territory. Two hundred years prior to its construction the Scottish had tried to establish an overland route across the 80 kilometres that separate the Atlantic and Pacific oceans and the conditions were so challenging that they couldn't.

Digging such an enormous canal was a task of obscene scale. It cost US$350 million in 1914 currency, and updating to current dollars (around $10 billion) doesn't quite convey the ambition involved because our global economy is so much larger and richer now.[5]

The incentive to link the Pacific and the Atlantic was clear. The owner would be able to charge ships an amount approaching (but never reaching) the cost of sailing 'the long way' around the tip of South America. The US Government ended up owning the land in which the canal sat and ceded power to Panama slowly over the twentieth century. The canal became fully Panamanian only in 1999.

What this big channel between the Pacific and the Atlantic shows us is how far the price incentive reaches. The desire to present consumers with cheaper crackers does not just spur businesses to cut costs. It can reach out and carve a giant hole in the surface of the earth. Which is why it's so shocking that some of the time we deliberately disdain lower prices.

The luxe conundrum

So we've established that the price system is far more powerful than even Hayek seemed to grasp. High prices deter purchase but encourage production. Low prices encourage purchase but discourage production. Incentives not only provide a great balance in the forces that keep the amount of goods made and the amount bought roughly equal. They also spur great change.

But, of course, there is another way in which this all-powerful price system is flipped on its back and rendered completely laughable.

Ladies and gentlemen, I give you Moët Hennessy Louis – Vuitton (LVMH).

Duck off the Champs-Élysées away from the hordes of American tourists and towards the river. You are in one of the most expensive arrondissements in Paris – the *huitième*. Money piles up as you glide through this sliver of the city of light, and it piles highest on the Avenue Montaigne. This is serious *Rive Droite* territory. The paint is fresh, the architecture impeccable. Leaves on the trees glow with health and the engines of the German cars purr. There is nothing gritty about this part of Paris.

Nestled amid the opulence and leafiness, at 22 Avenue Montaigne, you find the LVMH headquarters. From this location the conglomerate runs a global enterprise taking in €45 billion a year by making a mockery of the system Hayek lionised and whose virtues we have sung. You see, LVMH is a luxury brand business. And what luxury brands do is turn the logic of price incentives on their head.

In 2018 LVMH made 10 per cent more revenue than the year before. Gross margin on its products was around 67 per cent of that revenue, and profit was around €10 billion.[6] The great well-oiled machine that is the price system can be hacked, and LVMH is hacking it each moment of the day. What they know and are exploiting relentlessly is that pricing things high sometimes has the opposite effect on humans to that which we would expect. High prices don't just deter us from buying, according to the magical and natural and efficient incentive system described in the previous chapter; high prices also make us crave.

Louis Vuitton handbag: A$6850.

Moët & Chandon 750 mL bottle: A$649.99.

Hennessy cognac 700 mL bottle: A$5500.

These prices affect our brain. Making something expensive doesn't always deter us from wanting. We don't behave sensibly like Hayek hoped. High prices make humble daily items – like a handbag – vibrate with desirability.

The neat little story Hayek told about conserving tin is right, mostly. But not always. There is a category of consumer item that humans use for show rather than purely for practical application. When we believe an item will reflect on us, and the way our friends, neighbours and strangers perceive us, high prices may suddenly become alluring. The high price makes us darkly plot and ruminate on how we can obtain the thing in question.

The reason we want expensive things is due to a phenomenon called 'costly signalling'. It's one of the biggest traps into which the human animal falls. And we fall headlong.

Like it or not, humans are engaged in perpetual competition that is ultimately related to our instinctive desires to procreate. We're all in the game. Even if we're trying not to play, others try to play against us. Humans want to look good and that goodness is relative. People want to show they are kinder, more generous, smarter, stronger, taller, more beautiful, more practical, braver, more determined, fairer or richer than other people.

In some domains the proof is easy to see. Height is hard to hide. Unfortunately, in many other domains our inherent goodness is hard to prove: we need to create some concrete evidence of it. To prove you're smart you can't just tell people – you need to get a PhD. To prove you're rich you can't just tell people – you need a Ferrari. And so on. The demonstration needs – and this is crucial – to be something that can't be faked easily. It needs to be something that would be costly to fake.

In the animal world the male lion grows a mane, while the females do not. A mane actually makes the animal hotter, and the growing of it expends valuable energy that could arguably be better used hunting prey. But the presence of the mane is a demonstration of the reproductive fitness of the animal and the lusher and fiercer the mane, the healthier and more virile the animal, and the more likely he is to find a mate and pass on his genes. This can't easily be faked.

Humans are like lions expending resources on their manes, or peacocks expending resources on their tails. We sometimes buy things *because* they use up our resources: that is, they are expensive. Our purchase shows we have the means to acquire them. This is in direct opposition to the typical price incentive, where the more expensive an item is, the greater the incentive *not* to purchase. The price system doesn't work perfectly in hundreds of product categories. Instead of conserving goods like Hayek imagined, we suddenly start flaunting them.

Now I know what you're going to say. You'll say that the quality at Louis Vuitton is brilliant. You have one of their bags and it's lasted for years. Blah blah blah.

It's true. Certainly the expensive item cannot simply be expensive; it must have some quality of which it can boast. Diamonds must sparkle, for example. Gold must glitter. But behind the gleaming disguise is another reason for the purchase: it shows off how many resources we have won over our lives. Often that reason is hidden even from the purchaser. And yes, there can be additional nuanced signals that our expensive purchase makes. Buying art signals taste. Eating at fancy restaurants signals gastronomic sophistication. Buying a Tesla signals environmental awareness. But these other elements can often serve as mere garnish on the underlying signal, which is in each case wealth.

Smells fishy

To illustrate how comprehensively the rarity and price of goods can distort their desirability, it's helpful to go beyond our current era. How about caviar? Eggs from the sturgeon fish are now a luxury few will ever eat.

I can find caviar for sale via gourmet food stores near me at A\$150 for a 30-gram tin. Beluga caviar, which comes from the beluga sturgeon, is even pricier. But caviar was not always fancy or expensive. It used to be stocked on supermarket shelves alongside tinned herring.

Early in 1897 'Russian caviar' was being advertised in the USA at 40 cents for a 2-pound can (just under 1 kilogram). It had no cachet as a status symbol; it was cheap and abundant. Caviar was served from the lunch wagons that fed the poor of Chicago for 10 cents a serve, the same price as ham and eggs.

As the nineteenth century closed, US sturgeon stocks were huge. However, they were on the brink of a precipitous decline that would make caviar rare again. As US sturgeons became overfished and scarce, so the exclusivity of caviar began to rise. In 1898 the *Los Angeles Times* wrote that the rise in prices would deter consumption, claiming '\$1 per pound can of caviar ... would keep most consumers off. There is, however, only a limited demand.'[7]

The *Los Angeles Times* was making the perfectly reasonable assumption people would stop wanting something when it got expensive. That's the sort of thinking Hayek relied on, and the reason the price incentive system usually runs well. But with sturgeon roe the inflation did not stop until the salty little eggs were a marker of extreme opulence.

Why caviar particularly? One reason may be that caviar is a visually distinctive food, and one you eat straight. It's not packed into a sausage nor blended into a smoothie. It can't be confused for pork or beef. It's also something that lends itself to being consumed publicly – often while drinking champagne – rather than something eaten quietly at home for breakfast. All of the above makes it especially suitable for costly signalling once it becomes expensive.

If you're wondering why we don't have luxury dishwashing liquid, luxury margarine and luxury toothpaste it's because those goods are consumed mostly privately and unlikely to be good candidates for costly signalling.

Remember the fancy sourdough bread from last chapter? When I was having guests over, I found it easy to overcome my qualms about spending so much on a loaf of bread. I would *always* buy that bread for guests. I could try to tell myself I cared about those people dearly and wanted them to have the finest breads. But a truer explanation for my behaviour is probably that I was engaging in costly signalling.

A conspicuous Norwegian

In economics a product where demand rises as price rises is called a Veblen good. The concept is the intellectual legacy of US economist Thorstein Veblen. A cantankerous Norwegian immigrant to the US, Veblen also invented the term 'conspicuous consumption', which has dominated a lot of critiques of capitalism over the last century. Conspicuous consumption is about buying things to be seen. Working hard to buy things that are enjoyed only as signals of wealth or taste is widely viewed as wasteful. The reason is that consumption by others can neutralise their benefit. If I buy a fancy car in order to show off, and then everyone else does the same, we've all spent many thousands of dollars and none of us has achieved our goal of elevating our position. We'd be better off buying something we enjoy for its own sake.

Veblen was on to this topic a long time ago. It's not new at all. But what is new is how conspicuously we're able to consume in the twenty-first century. Social media allows us to broadcast our lives to far more people than before. I have a theory – one I can't test – that Instagram is fuelling extra demand for travelling first or business class in planes. Where you sat in the plane was once mostly your private business – like what socks you're wearing. But social media changes that: if you're going to be posting snaps from on board you definitely want those snaps to feature the lie-flat bed. And I sure do see a lot of first-class travel shots from sportspeople and other assorted notables who crowd my Instagram feed.

Personally I buy the cheapest tickets available when I fly, since it's by far the best-value ticket on the plane. What you're really buying when you fly is access to the destination, and every seat performs equally in that respect. Paying $2000 more doesn't help you take off later or land sooner. Spending that much extra to become slightly more comfortable for a 12-hour international flight always seemed to me terrible value – especially when you consider how much more excitement or comfort that sort of money could buy after you land.

Flying commercial at all, however, is strictly for the lumpen-proletariat; true conspicuous leisure involves flying private. My social media feeds are also crammed with musicians and entrepreneurs posting from the narrow cylinders of private jets. This is the new status symbol. Entrepreneurial private jet owners are even finding they can make a bit of extra money without even taking off: private jets are in hot demand for photo shoots – all done on the ground. You don't even have to travel private to make it look like you did. After all, every incentive system can be gamed.

Scale

So we've established that conspicuous consumption inverts the traditional price incentive. We focused on some classically luxurious brands and items: Louis Vuitton and caviar and flying first class. But I fear that the impression I'm creating is that paying a lot for something is the preserve of the rich and frivolous. Which would imply that the extent of this loophole in the price incentive is limited. Your own personal experience might tell you it's not, and you'd be right. To see that the desire to pay more can affect anyone – even those who perhaps can't really afford it – we turn our eyes away from LVMH for a moment.

In Manhattan's Greenwich village, in 1994, James Jebbia opened a tiny skateboard shop. The name of that shop: Supreme. Supreme has grown from these roots to be a global presence that, like Louis Vuitton, retains enormous cachet. The difference with LV is that Supreme's image is very much youth and very much counter culture. Supreme sells skate clothing, of course, but in limited production runs. That makes them scarce and therefore desirable. You can at time of writing pay US$1650 for a Supreme hooded top online, US$950 for a t-shirt.

The intersection of people who are reading this book and people who buy Supreme is possibly limited, so I forgive you if you're drawing a blank right now. But get ready for a huge example of what they call the Baader–Meinhof effect: now you've heard of it you'll begin to notice Supreme everywhere.

The brand releases an enormous variety of goods. Some of them make little sense. In my opinion the epitome of the craziness was the chopsticks. Supreme marketed a single pair of plastic chopsticks, like you might find at a Chinese restaurant, imprinted with the Supreme logo. I watched one young consumer review them excitedly on YouTube. Please guess how much they cost before you read on.

The answer is US$170.

The Supreme logo makes the most unexpected goods highly desirable and very expensive. A Supreme-branded crowbar costs US$345.

The whole Supreme edifice is mystifying until you realise the way Veblen goods work. Supreme's mesospheric prices don't deter demand – they create it. (The mesosphere, by the way, is the atmospheric layer one higher than the stratosphere.) The signalling power of luxury goods is extremely strong and it works as well in the counterculture as in the heart of the Avenue Montaigne.

The loophole in brief

Let's review the situation: an accidental incentive has come along, and it's the price system. It has proven very, very useful. It probably helped humankind become what we are today. It works – most of the time – by making sure that we stop buying what's rare and start buying what's common. This is spectacularly useful because it means the market economy wastes relatively little of what it makes. By varying prices, merchants ensure the amount of something produced equals out to the amount bought, more or less. It's very efficient.

This system creates perverse side effects and problems. But we mostly manage them. However the system also has a loophole; there are times it works the complete opposite way to what we want. Sometimes high prices make us want to buy more, not less.

The incentive system on which our entire global economy depends has a bug in it. The price system spends most of its time coordinating efficient consumption. But it has a part-time job doing the complete opposite. It moonlights as an agent of chaos, coordinating wasteful absurdity.

When two competing households both spend $10,000 on luxury brands to prove their superiority, nobody gets ahead. This has the shape of an arms race, where two sides work to increase their relative power and are thwarted. Arms races, game theorists tell us, are bad for everybody involved (except arms dealers). They involve escalating expense for no gain to the participants.

Let us emphasise how extremely negative this is when replicated across the billions of people who make up the global economy. Much of our expenditure goes on basics we need to keep us happy, and we are certain that we would, if we could, spend more on education and preventative healthcare. But then a significant chunk of expenditure – many billions of dollars, euros, yen and yuan – is burned in a pursuit of having a product that is more expensive than other people's. At a global level, the misallocation caused by luxury expenditure is clear.

For the individual, increasing expenditure on costly signalling may be a relief. It will reassure them they aren't slipping behind. But every Benz that rolls its first mile and every Patek Philippe that ticks off its first minute contribute to making everyone else feel they are trapped in a bottomless pit of striving without ever getting anywhere. And if a bottomless pit of striving without ever getting anywhere sounds like an apt description of engaging in the modern economy, it may be partly because so much consumption these days is conspicuous in nature.

If conspicuous consumption were the practice of only one or two people, then this bug in the system wouldn't matter. But billions of us engage in it. The rise of the economic power of China – like Japan before it – has unlocked an enormous market for luxury goods and shown again that conspicuous consumption crosses many cultural boundaries.

Replicated time and again across all the billions of consumers in the world, this bug in our incentive system adds up to a problem. We're wasting money that could be better spent. The millions we spend propping up Supreme and LVMH could go towards things that would actually bring us happier lives – like preventative health care. But the incentive system we have chosen fits into the patterns of our brain in a way that makes that goal very hard to reach.

The price system should eliminate waste, not create it. Grow our civilisation, not stunt it. Make us happy, not empty. It fails at a number of points.

This begins to raise the question of whether we should try to do something about the bugs. Luxury taxes are one idea: they could raise some useful revenue and crimp the profits of luxury good makers. But will they deter demand? As we have seen, raising the price of a good can sometimes paradoxically increase its appeal.

Even those rice crackers, if you taxed them enough, could become luxury goods I would covet and plot to buy. I might even end up spending more each year on a few packets of 'luxury' rice crackers for parties than I now spend buying many packets of super cheap rice crackers for my own private gorging. And either way, the price system is creating unexpected side effects that are not necessarily good for anyone.

Chapter 8

Only the Fittest Survive

Incentive systems don't have it easy. They're not like ornaments made to be kept in 'the good room'; they're out there being used. And they are not used gently: bad ones die fast and good ones expand their domain. It's a battle of natural selection.

To examine this idea, let's start with an example of incentive systems in beautiful miniature. These incentive systems have been domesticated for human amusement. You're likely very familiar with these tame beasts: we're talking about games.

Games are not single incentives but incentive systems – the rules allow certain actions that get certain payoffs. And at the end there is a meta payoff – the ability to say 'I won.'

Think of games like showdogs bred for the Crufts Dog Show. It's not 'red in tooth and claw', but it is a competitive environment in which only the best can prevail. The selective pressures are hard; game designers refine their best creations just like dog breeders breed from their blue ribbon winners. Over time, the best games get better and more rewarding. Seeing successful games change and evolve is helpful; it reminds us that incentive systems are not static. In fact, it's no exaggeration to say that if an incentive stands still, it will usually be exploited and fail. The ones that survive are dynamic.

On board

The history of games is a human history and it starts a long, long time ago.

Chess is king among board games. It comes from India, where it was played around 600 AD, before spreading both east into China and west into Europe. Chess as we know it was not invented in one moment. It changed over time and place. In Europe, in the late middle ages, the final major tweaks were made to create the version we know now. It's a tale of a brilliant system triumphing as it evolved, and evolving as it triumphed, but it's not the tale we're going to go into here.

Chess may not be the most played game in the world but it remains the most respected. World championship chess is streamed live to surprisingly large audiences, and corporate sponsors tip in big prizes. At the World Championships of Chess in 2018, the purse won by Magnus Carlsen of Norway was €1 million.

But chess is laughably new compared to senet. Egyptians were playing senet when the Great Pyramid of Giza was just a blueprint. Its hieroglyph first shows up on a tomb wall around 3000 BC. A game about half the size of chess, with 30 squares and perhaps ten pieces on the board, senet's rules are more or less lost to time. Still, by gathering together pieces of old papyrus, Egyptologists have gathered enough evidence to suggest the pieces had to move around or across the board, with victory dependent on progressing fastest – a bit like backgammon or snakes and ladders. The game spread throughout the Egyptians' sphere of influence and archaeological evidence suggests it was still being played thousands of years later. Chess still has a way to go to match that level of longevity.

As we discussed in Chapter 5, the brain has reward pathways built in. Games tap into these pathways. A good game has a system of rules that cause punishments and payoffs, which in turns trigger surges of neurotransmitters in our reward systems. That describes all sorts of games, from chess to senet, poker machines to Candy Crush.

Part of the appeal of any game is the inherent enjoyment of playing, and part is the idea that we may be able to gain something from playing. In different games these elements are in different proportions. The structure of chess reflects arrayed armies meeting each other head on. One can imagine barons and princes sitting in their gloomy castles, inching their pieces forward into the conflict at the centre of the board, perhaps expecting all this practice in strategic manoeuvres to help them, one dark day, in battle. Over time the perceived upside of playing chess has changed – it's now considered a pursuit that extends one's intellectual capacities. Humans are attracted to games that offer a meta level – something they can use in real life, for example improved literacy. And one game in particular offers that.

In the first few decades of the twentieth century the English-speaking world was aquiver over vocabulary and spelling. In the US, the scholastic aptitude test for university admission – the precursor to the modern SAT – had just been invented. Its vocabulary questions were a gatekeeper to the world of the elite. Compulsory education was spreading like wildfire, while newspapers were now mass-market and affordable. That meant basic literacy was almost universal and no longer a social marker. But high-level facility with language still was. A newly prosperous America was awash with an unexpected bounty of leisure time and a desire to show off how learned it was.

Enter Alfred Butts, the man – nay, genius – who invented Scrabble, and his wife, Nina. (To what extent were the ideas of Scrabble to do with Alfred's bursts of activity, and to what extent Nina's methodical genius? A brilliant female inventor whose husband was the front for their operations would hardly be unheard of in the early twentieth century.)

Black Thursday

The history of Scrabble is a fascinating study in the design of a powerful incentive system. (Allow me to declare here a total lack of authorial disinterest – it's my favourite game of all time. By all means email and challenge me to a game.)

Born 13 April 1899 in Poughkeepsie, New York, Alfred Butts worked as an architect in Manhattan during the Roaring Twenties. The first skyscrapers were going up and there was plenty of work. Stock prices were at 'what looks like a permanently high plateau', said economist Irving Fisher on 16 October 1929,[1] proving again that making predictions is hard, especially about the future.

On Thursday 24 October 1929, Wall Street spilled. The Dow Jones Industrial Average – a measure summarising the share prices of large American companies – fell 11 per cent at the opening bell. After a brief rally the market continued to sink until 1932.

The plunge in value of all these companies marked the end of an era. The Roaring Twenties were about to be replaced by the Great Depression. Butts did not lose his job straight away, although many did. But he would not have been able to avoid the evidence of a crumbling economy. As US unemployment rose to 25 per cent, New York City unemployment hit even more staggering levels. Joblessness was visible everywhere. From *The New York Times* on 16 November 1930:

> *In streets where flow the business and industry of the city, one finds the unemployed on every corner, in almost every doorway where there is no activity. They saunter by silently and strangely enough*

they seldom beg. The panhandler of Broadway and Fifth Avenue is absent from these streets of trucks and factories. These men want work, and they want it badly, so badly they don't like to speak of their need ... 'White collar' workers – office men and women form a large part of the 500,000 persons who are walking the streets for work.[2]

In the 1920s in the US there was tremendous belief the future would be brighter and more prosperous. But evidence was now mounting daily that this confidence had been completely misplaced. The future was turning out to be a deteriorating spectre of impoverishment and human suffering.

In 1931 the axe fell, and Butts lost his job. He and Nina moved to a development on the outskirts of New York City – Jackson Heights, Queens. In moving, Alfred and Nina appear to have cut their rent bill enormously, from US$137 a month, recorded in the 1930 census, to $51 a decade later.[3]

Money was obviously tight. And Alfred Butts, in his search for an alternative way to make money, came up with one of the most preposterous plans ever. In the depths of the Great Depression, he decided to invent a new board game.

I can't imagine how that would have gone over at home. But there are no signs Nina was ever anything but supportive.

Butts began very systematically, producing a document entitled 'Study of Games'. His study did not lead him straight to Scrabble. This is not a story of a blinding flash of inspiration – that is rarely how great incentive systems are made.

Alfred considered three great types of games as part of his study. First there were games with pieces that moved – like chess and checkers. Then there were numbers games, like bridge and dice games. Last was games of anagrams.

Alfred had played a few anagram games with his brothers, and they had often been able to make the games more fun by tweaking the rules. This category was sorely underdeveloped. Surely, he reasoned, an opportunity lurked there. So, around 1933, he devised a game. Wrote Butts,

> *It is neither childish nor complex, yet may be played and enjoyed both by children and the deepest of students ... The true worth of a game depends, of course, on its entertainment value, but if in addition its players gain an increased vocabulary, a further knowledge of word structure and of spelling, it possesses something of which no card or board game can boast. LEXIKO (Greek lexikos, of words) is that game.*[4]

Lexiko was a total flop. It had no board, for starters. It also lacked the intersecting words that are nowadays synonymous with Scrabble. Worse, the goal of Lexiko was to change over individual letter tiles until you could make a nine-letter or ten-letter word. That could take a very long time indeed and would surely end mostly in frustration.

Nina and Alfred, playing the game in their Jackson Heights apartment, reached the conclusion anyone would: the game had deficiencies. But it had strengths too. Anagramming, for one, was a good idea. And Alfred made one other good discovery – figuring out the distribution of letters that would make a word game as popular as possible.

As a young man Alfred Butts had been greatly taken with the works of Edgar Allan Poe, and one piece in particular: a short story with the title 'The Gold-Bug'. In Poe's story, the narrator is friends with a mysterious hermit, Legrand. The narrator, Legrand and Legrand's constant companion – a freed slave named Jupiter – crack a code written by the pirate Captain Kidd. This permits them to locate and dig up a buried treasure chest.

For Butts the key to the story was the manner in which the code was cracked. Legrand deploys his knowledge of the frequency with which letters appear in English in order to solve it. (A hermit who lives in a hut on a small island, Legrand is nevertheless fallen from great heights of wealth and education. Let us not beat about the bush, this is not Poe's best work.) This code provided a spark that allowed Scrabble to eventually set the world on fire.

The mix of letters was crucial. Too easy and the game would lack anything for which to strive. Too hard and frustration would mount higher than feelings of accomplishment.

How to decide on the letter distribution that would make the incentives in Scrabble just hard enough? Butts reached for a fair sample of English language – the front page of the paper. This natural language sample set the game off on the right path.

In Scrabble, the letter E is sprinkled abundantly. Z, X, Q, J and K show up just once each – Alfred knew from seeing how infrequently they appeared in the English language that they needed to be worth the trouble. Balance is achieved via the points system, wherein the most useful letters are the lowest scoring and the most challenging the most rewarding. While E will garner a player just one point, rare letters are worth far more. Z is worth 10.

This finely balanced incentive design is common in successful games, and not just board games. When the NBA added the three-point line in 1979 the game was re-energised. (Now teams have figured out how to mercilessly exploit the points advantage of shooting from range, the game's governing bodies might be well served to move the three-point line out again.) Cricket likewise brought in the six and the four during the early part of the nineteenth century, providing reward at great risk.

As the Great Depression wore on, Alfred and Nina spent night after night sitting across the table from each other, playing the latest version of Alfred's game. If you think it sounds cute that the pair would sit across from each other and play every night, it's even more so when you find out they were hopelessly mismatched. Nina was far better at Alfred's games than he was. One evening she played QUIXOTIC across two triple word scores for 248 points and trounced him.

'I was the guinea-pig it was tried on in various stages,' Nina told a reporter from Poughkeepsie in 1955, after Scrabble had finally taken off. 'He'd come home at night and say "I have a new idea." Then we'd try it out and he'd incorporate it or discard it.'[5]

After these games, in conversation with Nina, Alfred made changes. He added a board. He changed the number of points for various tiles. He changed the size of the board multiple times. He changed the total number of letters. Each iteration was tested, and Nina's input was instrumental.

Eventually, though, in 1938, Alfred got another job. New York's economic malaise was over and buildings were once more climbing into the sky. His games had shown so far a resolute and complete absence of success. Any observer at the time would have assumed this would be the end of Alfred's dalliance with word games.

It was not. Nina and Alfred continued to work on the game. Whether Alfred or Nina was the brains of the operation, it was iteration that made the game successful. This game was not designed once and foisted on the world. In incentives, details matter, and only iteration will reveal all the details. A tiny quirk can make a game too hard, too easy or too boring. Scrabble was tested and tested until it was right.

Stravinsky's choice

In 1948, an acquaintance of Alfred Butts's named James Brunot took the game off his hands in return for a small royalty on every game sold. Where Butts was an inventor, Brunot was a businessman. He built up manufacturing operations for the game and slowly developed its market. Slowly. He sold 2400 sets one year; 1600 the next; 4900 the year after that.[6] And then ...

The myth preferred in all the re-tellings is that one summer, out in the Hamptons, the chairman of US department store Macy's played Scrabble and absolutely loved it. Upon his return to New York City, he marched down from his office to the games and toys section of Macy's to buy a copy of his own. Macy's, however, did not stock the game. The chairman was furious. He placed an enormous order and after that the marketing machine of one of America's most powerful retailers swung into action. Within a year or two, sales were up 50-fold. An overwhelmed Brunot decided to sell the rights to a major game company, Selchow & Righter. In 1953, over a million copies of Scrabble were sold. The game had become a pop culture phenomenon on an almost unprecedented scale. This was like Pokémon Go, but without the disappointing fizz-out.

Like Pokémon Go, Scrabble was all over the press. It was described as the 'game rage' sweeping the country in a 'tremendous vogue'.[7] Small stores were taking out press ads to inform the public they had copies in stock, and Macy's was running lessons each lunch time to teach people to play. An ad at the time proclaims, 'Families spend whole evenings with it.' The caption leans hard on a few choice sexist tropes to make its point: 'Businessmen addicts play it in the office. Housewives let the dinner dishes go unwashed. Nothing has hit game-loving America so hard since the first crossword puzzle.'[8]

But the use of Scrabble as a marker of discernment was still ascending. In 1957 *The New York Times* ran a long feature on the life of the composer Igor Stravinsky, who was at the time resident in Hollywood.

The piece – which, frankly, is a fawning hagiography – describes Stravinsky as 'a musical monument contributing so immeasurably to contemporary music that its whole character would reflect his personality'. Among the many illustrations is a photograph of Igor and his wife Vera engaged in a game of Scrabble in a room decorated with pricy artworks. If the photograph reinforces the idea of Scrabble as the pastime of the genius, then the text does even more so:

When [Stravinsky] travels, he takes along some dozen dictionaries representing five languages. One favourite sport is scrabble (for which he owns a special scrabble dictionary); another is the making of multilingual puns, invariably with extraordinary wit and aptitude.[9]

Where incentives lead

By the end of the 1950s Scrabble had both cachet and widespread appeal in America. Throughout the remainder of the twentieth century it also conquered the world (with a few tweaks for foreign alphabets and the frequency of letters in different languages).

The rules and payoffs of Scrabble – an incentive system – worked for humans everywhere. The game caused players' brains to sparkle and fizz with neurotransmitters, and in addition held out a promise of cultural capital: erudition and social mobility.

But those same incentives that drove Scrabble's success had peculiar effects when taken to extremes. Once the game began to be played competitively, the rules took on peculiar implications for those who played to win.

Serious international Scrabble is played with wordlists combining multiple dictionaries. The list of permitted words is now many thousands long. For example, there are 124 two-letter words, 1292 three-letter words and 5625 four-letter words permitted. You can play CWM and TAENIAE and many more bundles of letters that normal players tend to find unfair and aggravating. For top players to succeed, they need amazing word recall. But before you rush to look up TAENIAE, consider this: the trick, they say, is to not bother stuffing your mind with definitions.

Record scratch. Wait! What? Why learn words but not their meanings?

At the top level, this is no longer the vocabulary game that made people rush out and buy sets in 1950. The point is to exploit the rules within your capacities. There are no points for learning definitions.

The most absurd demonstration of this effect came in the finals of the 2015 Francophone National Scrabble champion. Two players made the final: Schelick Ilagou Rekawe of Gabon (a French-speaking country) and Nigel Richards of New Zealand. If there was not much chat between the two contenders at the final table, it was because Nigel does not speak French. He knows a lot of French words (which is to say, he knows all of them). But not how to pronounce them, or what they mean, or much in the way of French grammar. Nigel, a man with a prodigious grey beard, won the final, two games to one.

It is at the extremes of Scrabble that we see the incentive systems in sharpest relief. The champions are those who know how to exploit its rules. And what we learn about the incentives of Scrabble is that they don't specifically encourage a broadening of your vocabulary – just that you collect more points than your opponent.

In the end, although it's played with words, Scrabble is an optimisation problem that lends itself to highly mathematical minds. Winning requires solving several types of problems at once. You must manage space on the board like a chess player, while anagramming like a crossword solver, and calculating probabilities in order to figure out what letters are best played now, and which are best left on your rack to improve your odds on subsequent turns. At a competition level, all of this must be done while racing against a ticking clock. Tournament scrabble is played with 25 minutes on the clock per person.

The evolution of an incentive system

Scrabble's rules are set in stone, and the era of experimentation is well and truly over. Aside from a simplified Scrabble Junior, no further evolution in the game had made any traction. Others have attempted variations – Upwords and Options, anyone? – lost in the great morass of forgettable games. Until social media and smartphones came along.

By 2008, games apps were taking off. You might remember Scrabulous, a Scrabble rip-off that was played inside Facebook and was, in 2008, the most popular game on the whole social network. But Scrabulous got shut down, and in its place rose a genuine threat: Words With Friends.

Launched in 2009 as a standalone app, Words With Friends has proven its staying power. A new version – Words With Friends 2 – was released in 2017 and promptly rocketed to number one position in the app store's word game rankings, number one position in the game rankings, and, oh yeah, number one position in the rankings of all apps. Millions downloaded it.

May I make a sacrilegious suggestion? Words With Friends may fundamentally be a better game than Scrabble. I say this with some pain in my heart. I don't pretend the designers of Words With Friends are the equal of Alfred and Nina Butts. (The mutations that make an incentive design evolutionarily fit may be the product of chance rather than of an all-seeing designer.) Nina died in 1979 and Alfred in 1993. Neither lived to see a smartphone app. But I like to imagine that, great adapters and experimenters that they were, if they ever played Words With Friends they would have respected and enjoyed it.

Words With Friends stands on the shoulders of a giant, and is able to reach further. The core incentive systems of Words With Friends make the payoffs and punishments even more intense, and the neurotransmitters spark in proportion.

In Scrabble the biggest bonus tiles – the triple word scores – are far from the centre of the board. Words With Friends has bonus tiles that are far less benign. In Words With Friends, huge bonus payoffs sit awfully close to the middle of the game board. Controlling them is a strategic battle that begins from the start.

In this way, command of space in Words With Friends is even more essential than in Scrabble. Poor strategic play can be fatal from the get-go. (A common error in both Scrabble and Words With Friends is to assume your optimisation function should be about how high you can score in your move. It should not. You are trying to optimise the difference between your score and your opponent's score.)

Words With Friends creates an even more tense strategic battle than Scrabble, exacerbated by an even friendlier mix of letters. Despite the inestimable boost given by Edgar Allan Poe, it turned out Alfred's mix of letters could be improved on. Scrabble has nine I tiles, nine O tiles and four U tiles. Absent dedication to using them, they accumulate on your rack, making your life worse and worse until what remains looks like an ululation of despair: OIIOIUI! Words With Friends has a better letter distribution with fewer Is and fewer Os, and more S tiles.

The downside to Words With Friends' mix of useful letters is that seven-letter words are more abundant. As such, the return on playing them is scaled down. Instead of paying a 50-point bonus, playing all your letters at once fetches a 35-point bonus. The payoff for playing all seven tiles is admittedly diminished, but the reduced reward seems well offset by the greater balance of risk and reward overall.

This is the beauty of the core system of Words With Friends. But unfortunately that core system is marred by another layer that, in my view, ruins everything.

Words With Friends has, since 2011, been owned by Zynga, an app company that makes most of its money on 'slots' apps. It knows how to make games addictive.

In 2017 it added new features to Words With Friends such as Tile Swap, Hindsight and Word Radar.

I'll summarise the function of these systems like this: the app now all but tells you what word you should play, demoting the human to a sort of rubber stamp for the cognitive processes of the algorithm.

On the official Words With Friends Facebook page, I found complaints. 'I hate all these new features. I don't even use them because it feels like I'm cheating,' said a person called Susan Moyes in 2018.

Susan, I agree. Who wants to be a servant to a giant cyborg brain? Who would want to take on an opponent relying on that cyborg brain?

It turns out the answer is still lots of people. But that doesn't necessarily mean Words With Friends wins in the long run. Remember, the process of mutation that can confer evolutionary advantages can also kill a species. By diluting the game's challenge Zynga makes the game less frustrating for some people to play, but it has killed the impression that you might elevate yourself by playing. And that ended its social power.

Back in 2011 and 2012, celebrities boasted about playing Words With Friends. Alec Baldwin was famously kicked off a plane because he was so engrossed in a game he refused to turn off his phone.[10] But now? Not so much. You don't see the Igor Stravinsky of 2018 casually referencing their games of Words With

Friends. Nobody believes you're going to make yourself brighter using Word Radar.

Zynga's designers may know what they're doing in the short run. But in the long run? I fear Words With Friends has evolved itself into a dead-end where it provides more bursts of neurotransmitter sensation and fewer perceived chances for self improvement. In that space it has to compete against apps like Candy Crush Saga and will likely be crushed mercilessly.

I want to finish this chapter with the tale of one last game that shows just how easily incentive systems can spiral out of the control of their designers.

Second prize in a beauty contest

Games can win the great race of natural selection for reasons rather different to what their inventors imagined. To see how, we shall pack away the Scrabble box and jump back in time to pull out another classic game of the twentieth century: Monopoly.

The earliest version of Monopoly was patented in 1903 by Elizabeth Magie, a committed Georgist. (Georgists were – and are – followers of the economist Henry George. They object to the way land is owned and spend most of their efforts advocating for land taxes. They are wonderful, kind-hearted people who suffer endless disappointment.)

Magie intended her original game to illustrate the terrors of a world where one person tends to accumulate all the property and bankrupt the rest. Her game looked a lot like Monopoly – a square board with properties for sale and rent, railways, a jail in the corner, a bank full of paper money. You got $100 every time you went around the board.

Magie named her creation the Landlord's Game, and designed it to engineer an outcome where one player rose to own all the titles, while the rest were bankrupt and destitute.

'It is a practical demonstration of the present system of land-grabbing with all its usual outcomes and consequences,' Magie wrote in an article on her game in 1902. 'Let the children once see clearly the gross injustice of our present land system and when they grow up, if they are allowed to develop naturally, the evil will soon be remedied.'[11]

Magie's game went on to be a hit. People actually wanted to experience the inequality Magie designed as a feature. They paid money to be subjected to it, and not in small numbers either. Monopoly – as it eventually came to be called – was the best-selling game in the mid 1930s (no doubt inspiring Alfred Butts, unemployed and at home in his flat in Queens, to keep experimenting).

Why is Monopoly so popular? Why do people want to experience the inequality that Magie detested? Not because they want that in real life. In real life total victory and crushing defeat would be too horrible. But in the artificial world of games, such outcomes are the bare minimum to get us interested.

Thus the evolution of games is an extremely useful model to observe in furthering our understanding of incentive systems. We can see how iteration is vital. We can see how the powerful incentive system squeezes out the weak. But do not confuse the evolution of games with other incentive systems. Games are tame – they win when they please us and replicate when they meet our needs. Other incentive systems must fight the race of natural selection like wild animals. Out there, they can thrive even if they are ferocious and frightening to most of us, or even if they're venomous to humans. These are the incentive systems we need to watch out for most.

Interlude

Dog

In 2011, I moved in with my girlfriend. We didn't necessarily know much about what we wanted from life. But we knew one thing for sure: we wanted a dog.

We started looking for one straightaway. Going pound to pound, shelter to shelter. That is how we spent our Saturdays for weeks. We peered through the bars of literally hundreds of cages, checking out the mutts society let fall through the cracks.

About half of them were elderly Jack Russell terriers and my heart breaks thinking of what happened to them.

But we were not to be the saviours of a tiny yappy dog. We had an idea in mind. Medium-sized, female, and not in need of really crazy amounts of exercise. We checked out wiry-haired dogs, poodle-coated dogs and sleek-coated dogs. We dreamed of getting a puppy, but shelter rules on puppies were very clear. If you got a puppy, you needed to be at home with it all day. No families with only working people in them were puppy-eligible, so that ruled us out. The dog we could adopt had to be at least one year old.

At the time we were slightly offended by this rule – did they even want to get the dogs adopted and save their lives? Of all the dog shelters, the RSPCA was toughest on prospective adopters. It demanded photos of your backyard and a cooling-off period before you could take a dog home. But all the shelters had a surprisingly defensive bent to them.

Most pounds wanted a declaration affirming we had a secure back-yard, and one even offered us a discount on the vaccination costs if we got a 'pet licence' (that is, took an online training module on dog ownership). More than once we told a shelter worker we might be interested in a dog only to have them suggest that dog was not a good fit. We were not driving up to these shelters in our enormous black Rolls-Royce while wearing Dalmatian-fur coats. We were normal people! But all the rejection had us second-guessing ourselves.

Around that time I remember reading a fascinating article about how animal hoarding is a major sub-type of hoarding, and how many people who are guilty of it operate their homes as animal shelters. There is an actual – albeit uncommon – phenomenon of shelter employees who think no member of the public can ever care for an animal well enough to risk releasing it into their care.[1]

But – mostly – the shelters and their staff are perfectly sane. They are simply trying to convey an important point: how serious this is. Shelters have seen far too many dogs bounce back into their care after a few weeks. They are done with letting people adopt on a whim. This is a kind of incentive system – if you want the reward of adopting a dog, you must show you're going to care for it. At the time it felt like overkill, but, having now owned the dog in this story for a few years, I think it is smart. You can't make buying a dog like getting a goldfish. A dog is not an accessory. It's difficult work and that work has to happen every day.

A lot of the work is on obedience training, and obedience training, it turns out, is all about incentives.

Lost dog

The shelter we returned to most often was called The Lost Dog's Home. It's an enormous institution in an industrial area. At night, after the big roller door clangs down, the brick factory walls of the area echo with barking from its rows and rows of cages. There were a lot of dogs there.

Some dogs would come to the front of their little concrete run if you spoke in a soft voice; they'd lick your hand if you put it through the cage. But most dogs stayed at the back of their cages, peering out, and some quaked in terror. Dogs did not normally end up here because of an abundance of love and joy in their lives. Finding a dog to adopt was an emotional marathon.

One Saturday in mid December – on a slightly dusty morning after a work Christmas party – we made the trek once more to The Lost Dog's Home. Into the first row of cages we went. Cage after cage of heartbreak, but no pooch we could take home.

Into the second row we went. Not right; not at all right … Wait.

In the third cage was a medium-sized dog. Female. One year old. Brown in colour, with ears resembling the muppet Rowlf.

This dog did something none of the other shelter dogs did. It not only came to the front of the cage. Not only wagged its tail. It also made eye contact. Two bright amber orbs looked up at us. (Spoiler alert: this book has been written under the unrelenting gaze of these same amber orbs.)

Where other dogs looked cowed and beaten, this dog jumped up and put its paws on the wire. Mouth open, tongue lolling out, tail wagging, bright shining eyes staring into ours.

The sign on the cage said: 'Curly Coated Retriever Cross. Age: 1. Name: Chianti.' We had both lived in households with retrievers. And as for Chianti? That could be changed.

We got our pet license, bought a collar and a lead, and came home with the artist formerly known as Chianti in the back of the station wagon.

A dog is a wonderful model for showing the power and pitfalls of incentives. I have learned an enormous amount about incentives from trying to apply them to my dog. Her feedback tells me when they're motivating. When they're confusing. When they're not aligned well with the actual task. When we've set up something she can exploit. When we need reward and when we need punishment. And she's shown me that sometimes you can get the incentive by cheating.

When we got our dog home from the pound, we soon realised she had missed a lot of training. All of it, actually. The dog's lack of familiarity with the world was so broad and so deep that we had to conclude she had been kept in a shed or garage her whole life.

Susie (as Chianti would now be known) was utterly unable to figure out stairs – when my girlfriend went upstairs, I remember seeing the dog go and look *behind* the stairs to figure out where she had gone. Ascending or descending was completely out of her capacity to imagine.

Evidence of a deprived life came in many ways. When I put food into her bowl, she would take one mouthful and then run for the back door to get inside the house. Somehow she had learned that the only way to get inside a house was sneaking in when the door was left open by accident. (To be clear, she was welcome inside our house. Her bolting just left me standing by a bowl of dog food, with her peering out at me from inside the open door.)

The saddest thing was her first toy. We threw it to her, it slid across the floorboards, and she just sat there. Was it the colour? The fabric? We tried the same thing with a couple other chewable things and she didn't so much as glance at them. She had no idea what a toy even was.

This was a dog that had experienced a deprived childhood. The first year is the most important one in terms of neural and behavioural development, so we were wildly behind. The saving grace was she had obviously never been abused. She never cowered when a human approached, moved suddenly, or raised their hand. Instead, she would wag her tail in delight, expecting a pat.

This dog had a lot to learn, and so did her new owners.

Treat that!

I thought I knew a bit about dog training. It turned out I'd just been blessed with naturally well-behaved dogs. I was about to get an intensive training course in how to train dogs.

If you see an expert dog, the owner will be controlling it with whistles, commands and gestures. You might conclude that these are the best things with which to train a dog. That is wrong, wrong, wrong. The best thing with which to train a dog is meat. Turns out training a dog without immediate incentives is a bit like running a company without paying your staff. It might be possible, but you'll struggle mightily to get anything at all done.

As part of the big push to encourage responsible dog ownership, the adoption of our pooch included a few free training sessions. So just after Christmas, the three of us found ourselves back in The Lost Dog's Home, on a patch of artificial turf. We thought the volunteer trainer would be schooling our dog. He was there to school us.

'Don't be afraid to use the treats,' said the trainer.

I didn't get it. I somehow saw treats as cheating, or like riding with training wheels. I wanted the dog to show me she understood the trick by performing without the treat.

'Treat that!' shouted the dog trainer, when my dog performed right and I just stood there smiling. I thought I was demonstrating the dog's success. But I was demonstrating my own failure. I was failing to reinforce the link between the performance and the reward. I was completely failing to use the power of incentives.

This is how classical conditioning works. Pavlov didn't end up ankle deep in dog slobber by ringing the bell *some* of the time when he fed the dogs.

Later – much later – when the action is thoroughly learned, the treat can be removed, at least some of the time. In the long run the principle of the poker machine applies – random payouts are more addictive than regular ones. At the early stages, though, nothing is more important than giving the treat. Every time.

In fact, the very first step of training a beginner dog is just standing there and stuffing its face full of treats. You need to start at the very beginning. Establish for the dog that you are a source of incentives, and that these incentives are tasty. Without that foundation you can't go anywhere.

The most important thing I learned in dog training was to grab a slice of super-cheap manufactured meat and thrust at it at the fuzzy brown snout in front of me, whereupon it would disappear immediately.

Sit Ubu sit

Imagine you're trying to teach a dog to sit. This is the first trick most dogs learn – it comes quite naturally to them. You can hold your hand just above its head and move it back, so the dog has to drop its haunches. At exactly that moment the treat should arrive.

Timing is everything. Incentives are used like a scalpel. Delivered at the right moment, they cut through the noise. 'There!' they shout. 'That was the moment that mattered!'

Nothing is easier than jumping to conclusions about how quickly your dog understands what you want. But dogs are not like us. Yes, you and the dog are engaged in something called a training session, where the objective is learning something, and the key concepts are actions, treats and rewards.[2]

And yes, to you all this is obvious before the lesson even begins. The dog, however, has no idea about any of it. All they know is that they are getting a lot of attention right now. It's possible – likely, even – that in the dog, the excitement of getting this attention crowds out all other brain activity.

Dog bandwidth is like dial-up internet connection at the best of times. When a human is marching around giving it lots of eye contact, emitting noises and holding smelly handfuls of delicious treats, that is potentially overwhelming.

As far as our dog is concerned, babble issues from my mouth incessantly. Now I want her to suddenly pay special attention to the sharp bundle of phonemes that is the word 'sit'? And, furthermore, I expect her to realise that this sibilant emission comes with an expectation of a lowered rear?

Hegel and Bertrand Russell can't even agree on the definition of meaning. To expect your dog to get the meaning of the word 'sit' at first is crazy. This is why promptness in delivering the incentive is so important. It's a complexity reducer and a meaning creator. Prompt reward demarcates the exact moment that produced the reward. (Pavlov's dogs were some of the first to prove this point. Pavlov called the concept 'temporal contiguity'.)

Remember, in the dog's brain, a treat might be related to any other stimuli in the room. There might be sounds and smells far more salient than the fact they just sat their bum down. Getting them to see the link between action and reward is crucial.

Action and immediate reward. Action and immediate reward. Repeating this is the path to a well-trained dog. And it is a lesson for incentive designers everywhere. Timing of reward is crucial for the action of neurotransmitters. Research shows that dopamine neurons fire hard when reward shows up earlier than expected and fire only softly if the reward is slow.

In every incentive we've looked at so far, we've seen that fine points of incentive design can make or break the whole system. The same is true of dog training. How to hold your body, how to get the treat out of the pocket, how to deliver it quickly, how to use your hands and voice – these are key factors. They distinguish a Cesar Millan type from the shmuck having their shoulder ligaments destroyed as their dog drags them down the street.

Aversive tactics or positive reinforcement?

Cesar Millan, in case you don't know him, is the world's most famous dog trainer. From extremely humble beginnings, he has built himself a multimillion-dollar empire including an Emmy-nominated TV show called the *Dog Whisperer*, loads of merchandise and a travelling live show.

But Millan is a lightning rod for criticism. Millan's dog training includes aversive tactics. You can find old videos online in which Millan appears to deliver small kicks to his dogs in order to discourage certain behaviour. While that is well and truly out of his repertoire now that he has perfect American teeth and his own TV show, he still advocates using some aversive training tactics.

To be clear about what aversive means, it is not advocating violence. It can be quite simple, like pushing the dog's bottom down to make it sit, or pulling back on the lead when the dog strains. It's basically anything that could possibly be construed as punishment, or anything other than a reward-based mechanism.

We have used aversive techniques on our dog. We say 'No' in a loud voice if she does something wrong. (Just this morning I left my empty toast plate on the coffee table and came back to find her head extended over the table and tongue flicking out at some marmalade residue on my plate. I gave her a stern talking to in my special angry voice and hope that will serve as a reason not to do that again.)

That's not all. We have also occasionally used a special collar that emits a spray of citronella oil if she barks. (At certain times of year possums invade our yard and nothing is more aggravating to the dog than possums, just out of reach.) That worked brilliantly. She still rushes around when the possums are there but the barking is gone.

We also taught her to walk on the lead by tightening it whenever she pulled. If you pull on the lead, young lady, the walk stops to a dead halt.

These have been effective. But have they been as effective as a purely positive system would be? I'm not sure. Evidence is mounting that positive rewards can be more effective than punishments.

Aversive techniques in human training are still very popular. The movie *Whiplash*, set in a music academy, is a paean to aversive techniques. The film depicts subtle psychological torture inflicted on a promising student by a teacher – not because he thinks the student is bad but because he knows the student is so good. The message: it takes a tough teacher to get results. The movie is brilliant, but its message is rapidly being overtaken by science.

As discussed, I have no particular desire to avoid aversive techniques. There's a lot of passion about this online, but I have no dog in that fight. All I will observe is that in my neighbourhood are a number of front fences that pose big problems. Behind the pickets is an angry dog. Barking starts as soon as my dog and I appear. Sometimes a little furry snout will pop under a gate and growl.

At these times, Susie gets revved up. She growls; she pulls on the lead; she huffs and puffs. For a long time I tried shushing Susie. I tried yelling 'No' at her. I tried yanking on the lead back in the way we'd come, and I tried yanking on the lead in the direction we were going.

None of these worked. But one day I tried to change techniques. I started something they call counter conditioning. Susie knows what fences have bad dogs behind them. She tenses up before we even get there. So I started feeding her treats before we even got to that point. As we passed the danger houses, the intensity of the rewards would increase. These were not just dog biscuits either. We used offcuts of our own meals and other super high-value treats.

Instead of projecting anger and disappointment, I projected happiness: 'Yes! Good dog!' Instead of punishing her for doing what I did not want, I was providing her another outlet. Focus on me, the treats were saying, and you get paid. I was substituting failure and punishment for success and reward.

Does it work? Let me just say that nowadays, when she hears a dog barking, the first thing she will do is look expectantly at me. She has learned the association between other dogs barking and the reward far more quickly than she ever learned the association between her barking and the punishment.

Not only that, I think it has basically reduced her nervousness around other dogs. When dogs pop up in the distance, she doesn't get transfixed on them so much. She can ignore dogs now – even ones that are a few metres away.

I suspect that all her problems were related to poor early socialisation. You will remember I described her benighted childhood, most likely spent locked in a backyard, never being trained and not learning to interact with any other dogs. She felt uncertainty about what to do when other dogs appeared, and she reacted in the only way she could think of, which is with aggression. Giving a bunch of treats has given her certainty. So when she sees another dog, her world is not full of doubt and rising anger – it's full of the expectation of food.

I would still use aversive feedback in certain situations. For example, I do not feel treating good behaviour is a great way to manage 4 am possum incursions, not least because it would mean standing out in the backyard at 4 am.

But the lessons I've taken from my dog have given me a whole new perspective on applying incentives. Don't expect behaviour change without them, and focus on timing – quick is good – and on positive reinforcement as an alternative to punishment.

Chapter 9

Self-perpetuating Incentives

When I was young, about ten years old, I received a chain letter. It promised great good fortune if I sent it on to eight more people (lottery wins!), and terrible misfortune if I didn't (dead relatives). I remember speaking to my parents about it. They weighed up the merits of letting me learn things for myself versus sternly interfering and shutting it down. In the end they let me make my own mistakes, and I sent on a few copies. I awaited the great good fortune promised. Nothing much seemed to change.

Games usually have owners and designers, with the ability to tweak and modify their creations, but chain letters are an incentive system that adapts without guidance. In that sense they're a bit like the price system – constantly evolving even without a leader.

Incentive systems that occasionally don't pay out when promised are not unheard of, but chain letters take that to a peculiar extreme. Chain letters' incentives don't pay out. Or they do so very, very rarely. Over 99 per cent of them have no payout at all and the rest are pyramid schemes where the money keeps flowing to beneficiaries only as long as new people are coming in. Payouts end soon enough.

That makes their incredible ability to survive and proliferate all the more astonishing. Because chain letters and their descendants still exist. Oh yes. And they have echoes in a certain very contemporary invention that we will get to soon.

The chain letter is an incentive that self-perpetuates. I'd had no desire to send oddly ominous letters to school friends and relatives before I encountered the chain letter. But once in hand, the letter itself begged me to pass it on, to pass the incentive to others. This is a precondition for collecting the mutations that keep an incentive system alive. When a chain letter must be rewritten by hand, it has great capacity to evolve. Each recipient can jazz up the stories within before they send it on, and a process of natural selection will diligently amplify the fittest, most successful such jazzings.

The letter I got was not of the pyramid scheme variety where each person must send money on to others in the system. Those letters were once the subject of a national mania in the US. In 1935 the post office in Denver, Colorado, was suddenly swamped with letters with the header 'PROSPERITY CLUB – IN GOD WE TRUST'. It promised that recipients would receive US$1562.50 if they sent on a dime based on the mathematic principles of the chain letter.[1] The letters spread throughout the US within weeks and before long they evolved to cut out the middleman, giving up on the postman and gathering in physical locations called 'prosperity clubs' where the process of enrichment could be rapidly sped up. Eventually the whole trend got shut down under lottery laws.

Traditional chain letters have evolved with the times, and twenty-first-century citizens are perfectly susceptible to the new format.

In the first decade or so of email, from the mid 90s to the mid 2000s, I got more than a few emails that promised me a payment from Bill Gates. This simple chain email became one of the biggest hoaxes on the internet. The original claim featured a lawyer called 'Pearlas Sandborn' who swore she was paid $245 for every email she forwarded, as part of an 'email tracking' system. And that's not all:

For every person that you sent it to that forwards it on, Microsoft will pay you $243.00 and for every third person that receives it, you will be paid $241.00. Within two weeks, Microsoft will contact you for your address and then send you a check.[2]

Ms Sandborn claimed she netted herself $24,800. Which is a ridiculously low sum, really, when you think about the incentives in operation. If she could have found 100 email addresses she would have netted more than that. And the numbers would skyrocket if any of those people sent the email on. If Sandborn sent her email to just 50 people, and five of the recipients each sent it on to 50 people and five of them acted on it, and so on, you would be up to $1.9 million in earnings just going four rounds deep. (Geometric progressions are way more powerful than our intuitions suggest. This is why chain letters can survive even with low hit rates.)

Microsoft soon published a refutation to this classic chain email. It's a hoax, the company said. And that put a stop to that.

Just joking. Ever since, the internet has continued to circulate versions of this email. It may have been a while since I last received one, but I checked the Microsoft's Answers website in writing this and it's brimming with page upon page of brand-new queries from people who just got the email. And these were the ones savvy enough to suspect something and check with Microsoft. 'I am not 100 per cent sure, but the person who sent this to me said he did receive money,' wrote a user under the name DarrenBanks.[3]

How can it possibly still be going? The answer is mutations. Recently, the word 'beta test' replaced 'email tracking' to help keep things sounding contemporary. And in some of the letter threads, Pearlas Sandborn became Charles S Bailey, Manager of Field Operations. Interestingly, Charles S Bailey is a real person and really was a manager of field operations (albeit not affiliated with Microsoft). His name seemingly got mixed up in the email when he forwarded it on.[4]

Bailey is a terrific example of a random mutation adding to the power of the email. Once his name was appended, anyone who searched for him would find a somewhat credible-seeming result that made them more likely to believe the email and send it on. And that's enough for an incentive system to become self-perpetuating.

The chain email asks you to do something to get a reward. The cost of doing what it asks is low enough that even if the reward seems unlikely, a small proportion of people agree. And on it goes.

There are other evolutionarily fit formats that make people propel things online reflexively, and without even the promise of material reward. 'Share if you agree,' is one, although people are getting wise to that trick. 'I'm teaching my students about the internet and I want to show them how many times something can be shared online,' seems to be one of the latest formats that people don't instinctively process as a chain-letter equivalent, or spam.

The chain letter, and all these other chunks of shareable content, show it's not hard to bring into existence something novel that provides an incentive for people to share and promote it. You can even get people to invest their own money.

It need not even be your intention to create such a thing. It might be you were trying to create something else and you accidentally create an incentive structure that is demonically self-perpetuating …

The cryptocurrency wealth fountain

Bitcoin is a so-called digital currency, or cryptocurrency, invented in 2009. It has gone from nothing to being worth a great deal – the total value of all Bitcoins in existence is $70 billion at time of writing.

It's being invested in and hoarded, traded and speculated on, and is often compared to gold.

Is Bitcoin a bit like a chain letter? Is there a hot bundle of powerful, self-propelling incentives that perpetuate the survival of cryptocurrencies like Bitcoin?

Bitcoin is, arguably, an incentive system in the raw. Effective and wild. What was intended and what we got are only lightly related. The original point of Bitcoin was to replace money. However, the effect was to create an asset like gold or stocks. The powerful aspect of Bitcoin is not necessarily the original vision but the incentives that were whipped into being and are now loose in the world.

Bitcoin's genesis can be traced back to an original white paper that was published on the internet by a person or persons known only as Satoshi Nakamoto. The first four words in the introduction of that paper are 'Commerce on the internet'.[5] Satoshi Nakamoto intended it to become a way to pay for things, a decentralised, peer-to-peer currency and banking system rolled into one. But Bitcoin's impact on commerce on the internet has so far been fairly minimal. Vast amounts of internet commerce continue to use a huge range of other transaction methods. Visa and Mastercard remain prominent. The best rough estimate of Bitcoin's market penetration in online commerce is 0 per cent.[6]

Where Bitcoin has excelled so far is somewhere else – as a speculative asset. It has created an investment frenzy not unlike the original prosperity clubs.

Bitcoins themselves are just computer code – files that sit on a computer and can be sent over the internet. The whole point of Bitcoin is making a system that allows these files to be spent by their owner, and spent only once. All Bitcoin transactions are confirmed and recorded on a large database (known as the blockchain) that is replicated in many places all over the internet. These are the technical details. But what Bitcoin really consists of is an extremely ingenious nested system of incentives.

The first layer of incentives come about because Bitcoin is designed to do away with banks and their role in confirming that transactions get where they're going. The problem with banks, according to the Bitcoin creator, is that they require we trust them. 'While the system works well enough for most transactions, it still suffers from the inherent weaknesses of the trust based model,' Nakamoto argues in the white paper. At Bitcoin's heart is a nifty trick. It pays people to confirm transactions. That payment encourages a decentralised, peer-to-peer system to take on the bank's role, and thereby replace a powerful middleman with a different system.

A traditional banking system treats distributing currency and confirming transactions as very different functions. Bitcoin combines them into one. People who confirm Bitcoin transactions are rewarded with new Bitcoins. This is a tremendously clever piece of work that makes Bitcoin a self-enclosed and self-reliant system – a möbius strip of incentives.

Nakamoto realised resources would be used in processing bitcoin transactions. Confirming the transactions requires computer processing power ('CPU time') and electricity and therefore incentives needed to be provided. While Nakamoto couldn't get the incentives to line up in a way to make his vision of a new system of commerce come true (at least not yet), he nevertheless provided incentives strong enough to create something worth billions.

Why does processing Bitcoin transactions use so much CPU time and electricity? Because confirming transactions is done by solving mathematical problems. All around the world computers are set loose on these problems, competing to confirm the transactions are legitimate. The only way to solve them is by applying computer power, and whoever solves it first gets the reward. The term 'mining Bitcoins' describes these transaction confirmations and the ensuing reward.

In the very earliest days of Bitcoin, people could connect their home computer to the system, leave it overnight to confirm transactions, and wake up with hundreds of new Bitcoins. These people used electricity running their computers to confirm transactions, and were rewarded for that expenditure with Bitcoins. Of course, the coins weren't worth much then and took up disk space. Many were mined amid curiosity and excitement and later deleted.

But many were kept. And that was vital in creating the second layer of incentives. The masterstroke at work in Bitcoin is in creating people with a stake in it. Where most such innovations would struggle to attract early adopters, Bitcoin not only won them, but turned them into stakeholders.

While for a time the promise of Bitcoins being useful was just a dream, it didn't take long to become a reality. Once enough Bitcoin users gathered together in forums, they began to trade them for money. It was fractions of a cent at first. But Bitcoins suddenly had value in real money terms. That made them even more desirable. Slowly, Bitcoins became valuable enough and widely enough known that they could be used for commerce. One early adopter, a year after the launch of Bitcoin, used 10,000 Bitcoins to buy two pizzas.[7] (He went through a middleman – the pizza shop itself did not accept cryptocurrency.)

Bitcoins were easy enough to get and potentially useful. This attracted people. But that was only the first step. As owners of Bitcoins, these online pioneers – including influential people in certain corners of the internet – had an incentive to spruik Bitcoin. They could make its value go up by encouraging more people to buy. This is not unlike a chain letter. You have no incentive to propagate the incentive structure until it lands in your hands. When you start to own Bitcoin, you become part of the ecosystem that propels it forward.

In this manner, in fits and starts, the hype continued to rise, until December 2017, when the value of a single Bitcoin topped US$20,000. The pizza guy must've been kicking himself.

Forking Bitcoins

By the time you read this, John McAfee may be dismembered. Mr McAfee, the man who invented the famous McAfee antivirus software, fell from grace at some point in the last decade or so. He moved to Belize. He was accused of murder, but he hasn't been found guilty. According to his tweets, he has 47 biological children. And he got involved in cryptocurrency in a major way.

McAfee has a way with words, making him a compelling person to observe from a safe distance. He has a Twitter account that oscillates from extremely funny to quite offensive. McAfee, who appears to be in need of funds, has become a sort of professional mouthpiece for the cryptocurrency industry. He touts the benefits of various new cryptocurrencies.

The price of a single Bitcoin peaked at $20,000 in late 2017. But before that McAfee made his big commitment. He promised that the Bitcoin price would hit $500,000 within three years.

'If not I will eat my dick on national television,' McAfee said on Twitter on 17 July 2017.

Yet, after a furious run-up, all the air has come out of Bitcoin. For the price to continue to rise, new buyers must always be found. For a while that was easy. But just like the original chain letters, the fervour could only be carried so far before it simmered down.

Mr McAfee's corporeal integrity is in real danger unless the incentives behind Bitcoin can generate another big round of hype. Are they strong enough to do so?

One of Bitcoin's great weaknesses is actually a key feature of its design. It's a peer-to-peer system, so it's slower to adapt than a piece of software that's owned by a company. Changing the rules of Bitcoin is generally extremely tedious.

However, Bitcoin can 'fork'. This is where a number of the 'miners' can agree to adopt a different set of rules to others and, in doing so, create a new, additional cryptocurrency that is operated under a different set of rules. That happened in 2017, when a group of miners decided they wanted a cryptocurrency that made the vision of Satoshi Nakamoto come alive – one that was more useful for commerce on the internet. They called it Bitcoin Cash. But their vision came with a compromise. To make the cryptocurrency easier to spend, it would have to become more centralised and rely less on a broad peer-to-peer network.

The legacy of Satoshi Nakamoto was hotly debated. Did he want Bitcoin to be peer-to-peer or did he want it to be useful as cash? Bitcoin clung to the former vision while the group behind Bitcoin Cash strived to achieve the second latter. The 'fork' took place amid a level of acrimony that was hilarious and also frightening to behold. A list of insults hurled at the users of Bitcoin Cash would take up the rest of this book. (If you've belonged to a political party, a friendship group or even an internet forum, you know how these schisms can be – intense to those involved and absurdly minor to those not.)

Whether or not they heard those insults, the 2017 forkers might feel a bit silly. A unit of Bitcoin Cash is now worth US$132 compared to a Bitcoin's value of US$3860.

DOGECOIN ET AL.

While Bitcoin tends to be slow to adapt, cryptocurrency generally is a hotbed of experimentation. Bitcoin was followed by many alternatives, including Dogecoin, which is an elaborate joke created in reference to a popular internet meme about dogs.

The number of active cryptocurrencies peaked at over 2500. Many are now worthless and no longer traded. Dogecoin, you'll be pleased to hear, is going fine and has a market capitalisation (i.e. total value) of over US$240 million.

Even as the lifeless forms of extinct cryptocurrencies are carted away, new ones are being invented. There's a cryptocurrency for every purpose, and there's no sign the flow of them will ebb any time soon. This, you will recognise, is the Butts model of constant experimentation and innovation.

And we need not rely on the diligence of one out-of-work architect to continue to create new versions. Many people are willing to try to create a valuable new cryptocurrency. The upsides are potentially enormous. The inventor will often keep a generous slice of all coins in existence for themselves, or alternatively may mine them in the early days at a low cost. If the invention goes on to be worth something, these pioneers can be looking at multibillion-dollar paydays. Satoshi Nakamoto is (are?) estimated to own between 700,000 and a million Bitcoin. At time of writing that's around US$4 billion.

So the next outbreak in cryptocurrency fever could well be in a coin other than the original Bitcoin. If a newer cryptocurrency ever comes to dominate – and it remains a big *if* – I'd bet on the one that has built in the most attractive incentives for adoption and promotion, and also some capacity to adapt over time.

Incidentally, it's worth noting here one of the aspirations of some of the more extreme cryptocurrency fans: a desire to destroy the existing monetary order and all central banks. It seems highly unlikely this will happen. Bitcoin is the best known and most widely used cryptocurrency, but its incentives don't currently seem strong enough to encourage us to get rid of our currencies altogether. Quite the reverse – now most people who hold Bitcoin do so because they hope to be able to trade it for a large sum of traditional currency at a later point.

So far no cryptocurrency has come along that could scratch the global financial system, let alone imperil it. Which is good news, really, because the financial shock of changing monetary systems would likely be extremely deleterious to billions of people.

But cryptocurrencies keep adopting new forms. Trying on new guises. As Alfred and Nina Butts showed, tweaking the rules is an essential pre-condition to finding an incentive structure that can survive and prosper. On the off-chance that a cryptocurrency evolves that is so powerful as to usurp the existing financial order, it would prove an existentially threatening example of how the most evolutionarily fit incentive scheme may not always be the one that's most beneficial.

The people who own these cryptocurrencies would feel smug for a while. But when the starving mobs arrive on their properties and tear down their walls, the crypto fans would begin to regret starting a process they could not in the end control.

It may sound far-fetched that the currency equivalent of a chain letter could end the world as we know it, and I'm certainly not predicting it. But neither would I put it past the human race to engineer its own destruction via an idle flight of fancy, animated by powerful incentives.

Chapter 10

Corruption and Rot

It might start with a mistake. An accountant puts through a false payment and nobody notices that the seeds of embezzlement are sown. A person discovers they can fail to do their job properly and still get paid and promoted. That's when an organisation's incentive system begins to be corrupted.

Many incentive systems rely on people to run them. Someone has to enforce, someone has to hand out rewards. Some systems, like the price system, recruit those people in an ad hoc and decentralised fashion – anyone who buys and sells is part of the operation. Other incentive systems rely on insiders to administer rules that apply to outsiders. In the case of colonial Ha Noi, the French bureaucrats are the insiders and the people who hunt for rats are the outsiders. The outsiders can corrupt the incentive scheme by finding ways to exploit it.

But nestled inside organisations, the administrators are not immune. Incentives can warp the people who are supposed to be their custodians. If those people get corrupted the whole incentive system gets corrupted. It stops doing what it was intended to do and starts doing something else entirely.

In this way incentives are prone to rot. Unless the system reacts to warped incentives immediately and keeps things assiduously clean, it allows failure to be rewarded. The decay will creep into the crevices of the things you value most and slowly eat them apart.

This chapter will show how the incentives of science have been eroded by the very institutions that are supposed to uphold them. And it will show that a good incentive system can't just be strong; accidental incentives develop fast, and a quick reaction is necessary. Fighting them means floating like a butterfly and stinging like a bee. Incentive systems never stand still, and the price of controlling all that insidious power is constant vigilance and frequent adaptation. But science is famously slow.

'Science proceeds one funeral at a time.'[1]

In 2018 the world of science saw a huge breakthrough. Cancer was not cured. But the discipline finally discovered a reverse gear. Dozens of papers by a leading researcher were retracted. These papers were mostly bullshit, and the scientific community publicly admitted it. They confessed that their most exalted institutions – august universities and esteemed journals – had been cultivating and selling bullshit.

You may be surprised to hear that, since one of the organising principles of the scientific establishment is essentially to not publish bullshit. Arguably the *raison d'etre* of the whole Enlightenment is to not do that.

So how did it come to this? The scientific community is a cohort of trained professionals using finely honed processes meant to sort truth from falsehood. It's designed as a big bullshit filter. All its incentive systems – p-values, publications, professorships – are meant to reward truth-seeking. Yet in 2018 we learned the filter had failed. The incentives had failed. And the institutions faced a very painful choice. Let the bullshit stand, or, by un-publishing it, admit to that failure.

They didn't make the right choices immediately, nor did they make them painlessly. But at least some made them eventually.

While this is good news, the admission that scientific incentive structures are failing came from deep inside the establishment, meaning the visible part of the problem might well just be the tip of the iceberg. The big discovery is not that science can retract bad research under pressure. It's that science could get so corrupt in the first place.

'Most published research findings are false,' claimed Stanford professor John Ioannidis in a paper in 2005.[2] Not too many people paid attention to that, because Ioannidis is a well-known gadfly, and because he was well ahead of his time.

Ten years later this claim was repeated, but this time it was far more startling because it came from Dr Richard Horton, head of esteemed medical journal *The Lancet*:

> *The case against science is straightforward: much of the scientific literature, perhaps half, may simply be untrue. Afflicted by studies with small sample sizes, tiny effects, invalid exploratory analyses, and flagrant conflicts of interest, together with an obsession for pursuing fashionable trends of dubious importance, science has taken a turn towards darkness.*[3]

Scientists are not bad people. Very few are easily drawn off the path of all that is good and holy. These people have principles, and most hold on to them tenaciously. Whether morality is innate or, as I suspect, partly learned by exposure to the right incentives in early life, it is a powerful determinant of how most people act. The problem is that the researcher who relaxes their principles can publish easily and get ahead of the researcher who is steadfast. Why? Because the incentives at play cause a major problem in the way scientists get promoted.

Scientists are lauded for discovering things, but not all discoveries are equal. Data that shows a drug did not improve cancer survival is unlikely to get you champagne in the lab and a front-page story. Everyone celebrates the publication of good results. And this is what we want too, right? We want scientists to make positive discoveries and then implement them to help all humans. We celebrate Newton and Galileo for what they found, not for what they looked into and realised didn't work.

If discovery is like digging for gold, we want to hear about the nuggets, not the spadefuls of dirt. But it's not always the best prospector who finds gold. The scientists who make great discoveries are lauded as brilliant, but we should also celebrate scientists whose work *could* create good discoveries. Whether their shovel comes up gleaming with gold or laden with mud is somewhat random and ought not entirely determine whether they become professors and win Nobel prizes.

In a moment we'll look closely at the way scientific careers work. It's a frightening situation that may make you very relieved you never took that Year 12 chemistry class. But first let's meet the researcher behind all those studies and papers that got un-published in 2018.

X-ray vision carrots, and other exaggerations

Cornell University is in New York State, way up, halfway to Canada from the city of New York, in a city called Ithaca. It's an Ivy League school, which means it sets high student fees and has billion-dollar investment accounts. The buildings were largely built of stone in a time before architects put function over form. It's a beautiful place full of brilliant minds and grassy quadrangles.

In one of Cornell's old stone buildings was the Food and Brand Lab. You may have heard of its work. It was behind some famous findings, like that serving food on a smaller plate will make you eat less, or that if the colour of food matches the colour of your plate you'll serve yourself more, or that if you label carrots 'X-ray vision carrots' schoolkids will eat twice as many of them.

Brian Wansink was the head of the lab, a position that brought him a great deal of publicity and credibility. His lab's studies were not only numerous and influential – they were also on fun and accessible topics that were meaningful for our everyday lives, like how to eat less and drink more water.

Professor Wansink is a lean, blond, enthusiastic man with a booming laugh. He had power, money and reputation. His work was published in many high-status journals, including the *Journal of the American Medical Association Pediatrics*. But one by one he began to lose publications, as they were disputed and retracted. Then he was found to have committed academic misconduct. Finally he resigned from Cornell in 2019.

Why did he stray? Some scientists may want the recognition that comes with major scientific discoveries more than they want the truth. And Wansink asked his researchers to find results that would 'go virally big time'.[4]

Wansink's undoing began in a manner so rich in poetic justice no fiction writer would dare invent it. In late 2016, he attempted to write a motivating paean to go-getter attitudes. It took the form of a blog post on his personal website. (This blog post is nominally deleted, but my goodness, the internet finds it hard to forget things.) The post is titled 'The grad student who never said no'.

Let's ignore for a moment the #MeToo implications of such a headline and focus on the science. In the blog post Wansink describes asking two young members of his team to look at an old dataset and see if they could find anything in it. One (a paid member of staff) says no, and he excoriates her lack of drive. The other (an unpaid intern) is relentless. She dices the data dozens of ways until she finds something. Wansink, in the blog post, celebrates her attitude:

> *Facebook, Twitter, Game of Thrones, Starbucks, spinning class … time management is tough when there's so many other shiny alternatives that are more inviting than writing the background section or doing the analyses for a paper … Yet most of us will never remember what we read or posted on Twitter or Facebook yesterday. In the meantime, this … woman's resume will always have the five papers below.[5]*

He then lists five papers he co-authored with the go-getting member of the lab. Wansink might be the worst kind of boss – refusing to acknowledge staff might face incentives to prioritise something above extra work – but the big problem is not his potential lack of management nous. It's his lack of statistical nous.

Like staring at a pinewood wall, the longer you look at a dataset, the more patterns you can find. Dicing a dataset 10 ways after the fact is not an acceptable approach to hypothesis testing, as Wansink was about to be reminded.

While statistics can be intimidating, used properly they are simply a tool to help identify phenomena that occur reliably, but not always, based on things we might see sometimes, but not always. Randomness means patterns could be present in the data. The trick to statistics is using them in a way that stops you from identifying random patterns as real phenomena. If you keep coming up with theories for a single dataset you're bound to find a theory that matches the random patterns eventually. This is what Wansink is congratulating his unpaid staffer on doing. The academic crime Wansink unwittingly admits to is turning noise into signal. The job of the scientist is supposed to be the reverse.

The findings Wansink and his grad student made were turned into studies like 'Low Prices and High Regret: How Pricing Influences Regret at All-You-Can-Eat Buffets'. Contrary to what most would assume, the paper concludes that:

Paying less for an [all-you-can eat] experience has a number of surprising consequences; lower paying diners feel themselves as more physically uncomfortable and guiltier compared to the higher paying diners, even when they ate the same amount.[6]

The paper measured many different combinations of feelings and prices at the buffet, and the fact that price, guilt and comfort showed a statistical relationship may have been chance. Note that nobody claimed Wansink was definitely wrong, but that he didn't have enough evidence to be sure he was right. The paper was later retracted.

That Wansink was brought down while giving unsolicited advice is ironic. Because some unsolicited feedback was about to make his life very hard.

After he published that blog post, drama accelerated rapidly for Wansink, starting with the very first comment on the blog: 'Brian – Is this a tongue-in-cheek satire of the academic process or are you serious? I hope it's the former.'[7]

This was just the first spark in an inferno of criticism. The next comment came from Robin Kok, a Danish academic: '[Y]our behaviour is one of the biggest causes of the proliferation of junk science in psychology and you are the one who should be shamed, not the postdoc.'

From there, things spiralled. The data-slicing, multiple-analysis approach turned out to be only the tip of the iceberg. The whole lab was tainted in more ways than you could imagine. It has since been shut down, and its presence deleted from the Cornell website.

The heroes of our science story are other researchers who looked into all of Wansink's research, on their own time. One of them, Tim van der Zee, a PhD student at Leiden University in the Netherlands, published what he calls the Wansink Dossier. It contains a summary of a huge list of Wansink papers and their alleged failings. This description of a 2003 paper gives you the flavour.

Wansink, B., & Westgren, R. (2003). Profiling taste-motivated segments. Appetite, *41, 323–327.*
Citations: 18

A range of inconsistencies with the statistical values. In addition, a range of reported values are impossible or highly improbable. In addition, there is a substantial overlap in the text with another paper: Wansink, B., & Cheong, J. (2002). Taste profiles that corre-late with soy consumption in developing countries. Pakistan Journal of Nutrition, *1, 276–278. These papers do not only share the same text; there is a wide range of odd similarities in terms of the data, while the samples are supposed to be different.*[8]

The dossier goes on for page after horrible page. One finishes it with the impression that at least some of the data in some Wansink studies is partially made up.

These academic failings matter all the more because Wansink's findings were being put into practice. In 2007, the White House appointed Professor Wansink to lead the USDA committee on dietary guidelines. His work, which promoted simple changes like making fruit more prominent at school canteens (known as 'Smarter Lunchrooms'), influenced policy at the highest level, as described by food policy expert Bettina Elias Siegel:

To date, the U.S. Department of Agriculture has spent $8.4 million to directly fund the Smarter Lunchrooms research and implementation, and another $10 million in grants to help schools put the Smarter Lunchroom principles into practice. The agency also now requires schools to implement some Smarter Lunchroom techniques in order to qualify as 'Healthier US Schools,' and the Obama-era federal rule on local wellness policies specifically informs school districts that at a minimum, FNS [the USDA's Food and Nutrition Service] expects [districts] to review 'Smarter Lunchroom' tools and strategies, which are evidence-based, simple, low-cost or no-cost changes that are shown to improve student participation in the school meals program while encouraging consumption of more whole grains, fruits, vegetables, and legumes, and decreasing plate waste.[9]

In a way it's not surprising Wansink's research was so well received. At its heart, his research fits neatly into our current preoccupation with life hacks. Life hacks are simple changes you can make to your life, and, as anyone who has been online recently will know, they are very popular subjects for articles on lifestyle websites. And life hacks that can help you lose weight are even better. There's an incredibly rich vein of demand for findings like his, so Wansink had a strong incentive to increase his supply of findings. He did so. Until it all fell apart.

Barbarians at the gate

What makes the efforts of van der Zee and his collaborators impressive is not that they found scientific malpractice, but that they made headway. Van der Zee's dogged work has drawn out of the woodwork other researchers who claim they pursued similar lines of enquiry on other researchers in other fields, discovered big problems, and then found themselves butting their head against a brick wall. Universities and journals closed ranks, protecting their own.[10]

Bad research, it turns out, is everywhere in science. The first field to come face to face with its demons was psychology. Psychology went through, and continues to endure, a well-publicised 'crisis of replication.' It has been shown that many previous findings cannot be replicated. This raises a question. If the finding does not hold up now, was it ever true? The answer is unclear. As psychologists have gone back through the vault of old findings from the scientific literature they have shown that many famous findings are false and that some findings verge on scientific malpractice. But retracting old findings is very rare.

Science has a filter process called 'peer review' that is supposed to engage experts to make sure only the truth gets to be published. If the claims about the extent of false findings are true, peer review is obviously deficient.

Bad research is getting published, and that's terrible news because it's awfully hard to erase once it's out there. You might expect the burden of proof would remain on the person making a scientific claim. But once a paper is in print, authors seem to be able to shrug off that burden all too often. The fact of publication seems to stand as the defence.

Nick Brown is a researcher who worked with Tim van der Zee in investigating Brian Wansink. In 2017 he described the situation with science like this:

Right now we have all the guards on the outside of the castle in the form of peer review; when that fails, and something bad slips past, often nobody has much of a clue what to do.[11]

The standards that must be met to justify retracting a paper are higher than the standards required to reject a paper from publication in the first place. That approach may have had at least some logic back when papers were literally on paper, and there was no way to communicate to anyone holding the original publication that the contents had subsequently been shown to be deficient, but it makes no sense now when everything is online and it's easy to immediately edit or un-publish something. Getting a paper into a journal should not be enough to make it immune to criticism and review.

Here we observe a pattern we find time and again in corrupt incentive systems. Once the system becomes sufficiently corrupt, once the rules are being bent by insiders and the payoffs distributed to them, the system becomes unable to self-correct.

The rewards of publication are enjoyed by the author and publisher alike, and the glow spills over onto the university that employs the authors. These organisations are supposed to uphold scientific integrity. But they are reluctant to retract bad papers. Sometimes they wait until the outcry raised by outsiders forces them to.

Outsiders normally have no incentive to tear a corrupt organisation or person down – beyond their sense that things should not have gone so horribly wrong. (This is another example of how morality can provide a final guidepost even when incentives have fallen into disarray!) But without incentives few outsiders will be spurred to the action required to effect change. When a group of unpaid critics assembles, it's often a sign that things have gone completely beyond the pale.

If you find your industry or organisation or system besieged by outsiders saying you're doing things wrong, your incentive will be to deny and cover up. (Shout-outs here to professional cycling and to the Catholic Church.) By that stage the corruption is generally so ingrained that eradicating it will cost many people their reputations and livelihoods. If you're senior in that organisation, and especially if you're late in your career, the cost of tearing everything down and starting again must seem very high compared to the cost of a few more years of justifying the existing paradigm.

Tim van der Zee may be an academic but he is junior enough in the world of science that his work on exposing the errors of Wansink can be seen as coming from outside its structures. When an incentive system relies on angry outsiders for correction, it's a failing system. The incentives no longer work as intended but are being exploited by the insiders.

If the incentive systems of science worked properly, the first questionable paper a researcher tried to publish would be stopped in its tracks; they would learn that the only way forward is to do research properly. But instead they learn they can get bad research into the literature, and that it's very unlikely to be retracted. If retractions are rare, taking the gamble of publishing quick and dirty research is potentially positive. A high-profile celebrity professor can be paid a fortune – probably somewhere between the average Cornell professor salary of US$170,000 a year,[12] and the salary of the highest-paid professor in the US: $4.3 million.[13] A top professor would very likely make millions of dollars over their career.

Wansink would still be making a professor's wage were it not for a handful of outsiders who stood up for good scientific practice. If his profile were a little lower, his mistakes a little less egregious, or even if he hadn't published that blog post, he may not have attracted such opposition and could still be exploiting the broken incentive structures of science.

Is Wansink an outlier? Much of the coverage of his behaviour has focussed on the man, not the systems that enabled him. He *is* an outlier in one way, because he's been caught and publicly discredited. But his behaviour is probably not unusual – it is one of the perverse side effects encouraged by the incentives of science. I recommend keeping an eye on scientific malpractice stories for the next few years as there will almost certainly be more exposés to come.

It's a long way to the top

To progress in a science career, you must get your scientific papers into journals. It's publish or perish, and perishing is very common. A science career has what's called a 'tournament' structure, with many contenders at the entry level and few winners at the top. It shares this structure with law firms and professional sport – not everyone can make it. Many must be pushed out.

In science the fat bottom of the pyramid is partly caused by another incentive system. Funding schemes reward university departments for each new PhD candidate they recruit.

An excess of bright, optimistic young people enters the tournament. They almost certainly misunderstand how brutal the tournament structure is. The powerful people in their university are professors, and all of the professors have PhDs. The link between a PhD and a position of power is established in the mind of the average student, and few realise how many PhDs work outside academia.

Between 2010 and 2016 over 430,000 students began postgraduate research degrees in Australia (e.g. a PhD or a Master's by research). In that same period 65,000 completed such degrees.[14] So far more than half drop out.

The hardy survivors may think they have it made, but a new horrible truth now faces them: there are more junior academics than senior ones. One 2018 study measured the 'half life' of academic careers in ecology, astronomy and robotics. Half the published researchers had dropped out within five years. This is a far faster rate of attrition than in the past. The biggest fall is in astronomy, which, in the 1960s, retained half its scientific workforce for 37 years.[15]

To aid the process of dropping out, life in science is hard. It's hard not only in the way you might want – that is, intellectually. It's also rife with bullying,[16] poor pay, bad hours and inferior management quality.[17] In a tournament structure, survivors are often comfortable with the suffering the structure inflicts on those further below. In part this is because they are survivors and believe the conditions select for high-quality character traits. The competitive dynamics also create no incentives for kindness. Tournament structures are unpleasant; even those who seem to be winning can drop out.

Take Douglas Prasher. Prasher is an American biologist who did groundbreaking work in bioluminescence. He was the first to successfully clone the gene for green fluorescent protein. Prasher willingly shared his work with other scientists. Yet in 2008, when a Nobel Prize for Chemistry was awarded for foundational work on bioluminescence, Prasher was nowhere to be seen. The prize went to the people Prasher had shared his discovery with. By that time Prasher had fallen out of academia and was being paid US$8.50 an hour driving a courtesy shuttle for a Toyota Dealership.[18] Sometimes, it seems, in a science career you can both publish *and* perish.

To survive, aspiring academics must publish, publish more than their peers, and publish in higher-status journals. This is not an environment that rewards careful progress, collaboration and generosity. Instead, there are strong incentives to hoard data and amp up results to try to get multiple published papers out of each experiment.

Science careers require a huge investment. You need to study an undergraduate degree for three or four years. Then a PhD, which can take another three, four, five or six years. Once this investment is made, it may be too late to reinvest in another career. In these conditions the incentive to juice up a result and publish something eye-catching but borderline untrue becomes intense.

The institutions of science – all the scientific standards, careful review processes and esteemed journals – are in theory set up to circumvent this incentive. They should be the gatekeepers holding dodgy science out. But too often in practice those institutions – most notably the system of journals – function as enablers.

Periodical power

You may have heard of academic journals like *Nature*, *Science*, the *New England Journal of Medicine* and the *BMJ* (formerly the *British Medical Journal*, it followed KFC in going to a purely acronymic name).

These journals are not only a way for academics to get their research noticed, but also provide credibility within their field. If your paper makes it into *Nature*, you win the esteem of your colleagues, and your chances of a long, happy, well-remunerated career in science go through the roof.

How does *Nature* decide what to publish? It culls lots of papers and (after they pass peer review) prints only ones that are especially exciting. Attention is scarce these days, with so much constantly being published, and getting someone's attention is a powerful reward.

But a system in which journals publish mainly just the exciting results is a problem. If you study T-cells to see if they respond to large doses of rituximab, and nobody expected they would, and they didn't, your finding is not exciting. It's boring. This so-called 'null' result is hard to publish, and certainly hard to publish in places where a benefit might accrue to a scientist's career.

The big journals, of course, have the opportunity to undo the bias towards exciting discoveries by publishing null results. But their credibility and prestige is in large part based on the fact that such journals are where you publish new or surprising or, better still, groundbreaking findings.

The upshot of this bias is that negative results are unloved by scientists and tend to get put in a file drawer rather than published.

Imagine many studies are done on a psychological intervention. They all show it has no effect. None of these studies are published. The literature therefore has no content on this intervention. A scientist decides to do an experiment to test the intervention, and thanks to random variation the results of the experiment show the intervention works. The scientist publishes the paper and receives plaudits for the discovery and there is nothing to show the results should be questioned. This is what we call a 'false positive'. A positive result has come from a perfectly valid scientific approach – note the result was caused by random variation, not malpractice – but the effect is not reliable in the real world. The bias to positive results is therefore a disaster for science.

Across all fields of science, millions of studies are being conducted that will likely never see the light of day. Because not only are there incentives for journals to publish only positive results, but for individual scientists, there are plenty of incentives to not submit negative results for publication in the first place. Writing up your results is hard. The process of submitting to a journal is even harder. You have to keep results quiet in advance, or they won't be published. Sometimes you even have to pay the journal to publish it.

What's more, you have to endure the process of peer review. Peer review employs unpaid and anonymous reviewers and grants them tremendous power to demand changes to a paper, or inhibit publication. Peer review is worth a book all its own.

Making gatekeepers anonymous, unpaid and powerful ... and having them hand-picked from among your potential competitors? That is about the worst conceivable approach.

Peer review has many enemies, and one of the most famous is Ron Davis. Davis is the director of the Stanford Genome Technology Center and he had his formative experiences in the Human Genome Project, which made its findings known simply by putting them on the internet. The project demanded that every sequence of base pairs had to be up within 24 hours of discovery. Davis, who was nominated as one of the greatest inventors of our age,[19] has ever since abhorred delay and its corrosive effect on the scientific process.

'I'm not very happy with the review process today,' Davis said in a 2016 speech.

I only get about one review every ten years that actually helps the paper ... As far as I can tell people who get reviews send them to their first-year graduate students and the graduate student has to come up with some criticism and some suggestions for some additional experimentation to show that they read the paper.[20]

Davis can see clearly the incentives for the senior researcher – who will, mind you, often be reviewing this work anonymously: get the thing done with a minimum of effort by handing it over to someone else. The incentives on the poor overworked grad student to whom the task falls are different: try to impress your boss by demonstrating a capacity to think critically. Peer review is one of the fundamental gatekeeping institutions of 'good science', but the incentives involved in traditional peer review are not conducive to doing it in the way it was envisaged, and that further limits the value of publishing in journals.

The reliance on formal pre-publication peer review could be reduced. Journals could decide to put less stock in the recommendations of reviewers, or even forego it sometimes. Post-publication review and revision could become a greater part of the scientific process.

The lesson of Wikipedia is that post-publication review and revision draws a huge number of eyes and is actually a fairly effective process for identifying and correcting error. I'm not suggesting that anyone should be able to edit a journal article after publication. But post-publication feedback and iteration – drawing on a wider group – could be superior to the current model.

Anyone aghast at the idea that Wikipedia-esque processes might improve the current processes of science should remember that Wikipedia was expected to be a disaster but very much isn't, while science is expected to be nearly perfect and very much isn't. The wisdom of the crowd should not be underestimated. Crowd-sourced quality filtering is also certainly more democratic than elite filtering by a few editors and peer reviewers.

Indeed in some fields of science – especially physics and mathematics – an online service called arXiv already allows academics to pre-publish their papers and collect feedback from a wide audience. Most do that even as they go through peer review for formal publication in the kind of journals that will help them get promoted. Others let their papers remain on arXiv and never pursue formal publishing.

Big money at stake

In 2012, Harvard Library complained that subscribing to journals was getting too expensive.[21] Institutional subscriptions can cost libraries tens of thousands a year, and there are thousands to subscribe to. That can start to get uncomfortable, even for the university with the world's richest endowments.

It also feels unfair. Universities pay millions of dollars a year to enormous publishing companies to access research their own staff produced. Paying to create research and then paying again to access it feels crazy, and especially galling when the research has likely been publicly funded. Big publishing companies are highly profitable – Elsevier, a Dutch information and analytics company that represents over 2500 journals worldwide, made over £2.5 billion (A$4.76 billion) in revenue in 2018, with a profit margin of 37 per cent.[22]

The good news is academic journals and their dodgy incentives are now under siege. Open access journals – which are free to read – are now publishing a greater share of total research output. What's more, a powerful coalition is assembling to support them.

In Europe, 13 national funding bodies are now insisting any research they fund be published in an open access journal.[23] It doesn't solve all the incentive problems in academia, but it does at least break the hold of the most powerful journals and create an opportunity for wider change.

What's notable is that such a change was only brought about by a large group of powerful European research funding bodies. This is not something one research funder could do alone. But once the idea had momentum other research funders piled on. The Bill and Melinda Gates Foundation has now also demanded that research it funds be published only in open access journals.

Bill Gates and half the European Union banding together to break the publishing cartel is the exact sort of heavy push you need to destroy an entrenched incentive system. The role of top journals in science had become so ingrained that nobody could break with them on their own. The shift to non-paywall journals could bring with it an opportunity to shake up some of the other negative incentives that many consider a problem.

Cleaning up your own messes

The good news about science is that it is self-correcting – sometimes. Wansink's retractions are a pleasing sign. But some of his papers were in the literature for years. Is that good enough? Have we moved on at all from Max Planck's quip about science progressing by mortality? Planck, a theoretical physicist, never actually used the famous expression 'Science progresses one funeral at a time.' He said this instead:

> *A new scientific truth does not triumph by convincing its opponents and making them see the light, but rather because its opponents eventually die, and a new generation grows up that is familiar with it.*[24]

This, I'd argue, is both true and terrible. Is it possible to come up with a way for science to 'fail fast', like they say in Silicon Valley? Is it possible to get scientists to pivot with agility, changing their minds and admitting their errors when confronted with the evidence, instead of clinging to dogma and prestige until the grave?

Back in the early days of the Enlightenment, one of the key institutions of science was the freshly invented Royal Society – a collective of men with sufficient leisure time and intellect to take an interest in science. In 1665, shortly after the society was formed, they invented the scientific journal as we know it: 'Philosophical Transactions of the Royal Society'.

The first edition of that journal included 'A Narrative Concerning the Success of Pendulum-Watches at Sea for the Longitudes',[25] which reported on the successful use of these timepieces in navigating to the Cape Verde islands off the west coast of Africa. Now, remember

Chapter 1? The British were still desperately working on the problem of ascertaining longitude 100 years later than this journal article. It may be concluded the timepieces were not exactly as reliable in navigation as the journal article implied. Why write them up so soon? The author admits in the paper that he has patented the watches in question. This may indeed be evidence the scientific literature has been polluted by bad incentives since the start.

Over the 350 years since, surprisingly little has changed in publishing even as science has been transformed.

Back then, publishing findings in a journal was a new and exciting best practice. If findings remained unpublished or published findings were erroneous, only the work of one or two aristocrats would be led astray. But we can aim much higher now, and we need to because science now is very different. Tens of thousands of research workers labour away around the world on major diseases like cancer and AIDS. When research is not immediately publicised, progress slows and work may be wastefully replicated. With so many people involved, the costs of anyone being unaware of the latest findings – both positive and negative – is enormous.

Timeliness is now key. Here we can see a contrast between the price system and science. Whereas the price system updates itself dynamically and constantly, the scientific literature is extremely slow to change. That is terrible for the incentive structures. When failure is allowed to stand, it is rewarded. A system that self-corrects slowly is a failed system.

If you rely on retractions that can happen only after publications are proven to be rotten to the core, you are doomed to prolonged waste and repeated scandal. If you make publishing small, negative findings a slow and painful process they won't come to light. Both publishing and retracting need to be faster for the incentives of science to operate properly.

I'd argue science desperately needs a new system of journals, a new system of career progression and a new system of peer review. But more than that, it needs that same speed of adaptation at a meta level. The people who operate in the incentive systems of science will constantly be tempted to divert from the purest course. What's needed is a system that will help them get back on course as quickly as possible.

Let many rich papers be published, and let their strengths and weaknesses be seen. Let them adapt in response to criticism. Make the scientific literature a bit more dynamic. Give it a bit more to-and-fro. Make it so that being considered a good scientist depends not on avoiding criticism but on responding positively to criticism. This is a set of incentives that will help make science better.

Chapter 11

Justice

How do so many millions of us live in such close quarters in some semblance of harmony? How do we keep anarchy at bay? Rules, and the power to punish transgressors.

The justice system – and this is no exaggeration – holds civilisation in place. Civilisation is itself a series of agreements. We agree to give up the chance to murder in order to not be murdered ourselves. We agree to not take other people's things in order to not have our things taken, and so forth. These agreements are mutually beneficial, but also fragile. Incentive systems help keep them intact by providing strong encouragement for people to do the mutually beneficial thing.

By promising punishments for transgressions we aim to shift behaviour from its natural state – featuring some unwanted level of selfishness and violence – to a more benign equilibrium. But we need to have confidence that any transgressions will be punished, and to do so we rely on professionals to enforce these incentive systems.

Incentives that provide justice can be informal (for example, in a hypothetical small society of a few hundred, justice could be served by way of retribution). But in modern societies justice is far more often formal. Big books of law set down what's allowed and institutions enforce those laws, which is good, because there are far more different types of interaction than there were in earlier periods of history and the number of people with whom you might interact is exponentially higher. For a species that lives in cities and interacts electronically as well as physically, simple systems of retribution cannot meet the challenge.

The incentives for justice are mostly punishments – a very different situation from handing out rewards. People will come to claim their carrot but they flee from the stick. Reward and punishment may be conceptually similar; one is just the inverse of the other. But this difference creates completely different requirements when it comes to administering them.

The work of applying punishments rapidly becomes about managing the people who are supposed to administer them. You can't wait in an office and hope wrongdoers hand themselves in. Bureaucrats who seek wrongdoers must be mobile and empowered, which is why police get cars and weapons. The practicalities of administering punishments become one of most important features of an incentive scheme designed for justice. And as we'll see, these complex practical systems leave many opportunities for incentives to break down; it's very difficult to supervise bureaucrats who have cars, weapons and substantial discretion in how to do their jobs. Without close supervision, administration of punishments tends to be swifter to corrupt than the administration of rewards. All the rank and formality in our justice systems, from the uniforms on police to the wigs on judges, represent our society's attempts to create enough structure to contain this natural tendency to slide.

But in many cases uniforms and badges are not enough. According to Transparency International, societies around the world perceive the police force as equal to the *other* most corrupt institution: elected officials.[1]

When incentives in a justice system break down, two things happen. Firstly, our natural human desire for justice is thwarted. (This desire is deeply rooted. Studies have shown animals have a desire for fairness,[2] which makes sense if you think about the fact that so many animals live successfully in social groups.) And secondly, our society regresses from the civilised state that our laws were so ambitiously written for. There's an irony here that we must have incentives to make the world a more just place, yet these incentive systems only need a nudge from their trusted administrators to become a source of terrible injustice.

In this chapter we're going to look at the justice system via two examples: one in which the incentive is very clear and upfront, and another in which it's all too easy to imagine incentives don't interfere at all.

Reward offered

Picture the word WANTED in bold-type above a grainy picture and a fat reward. The wanted poster is one of the most iconic and obvious uses of incentives in our culture. This is not a hidden incentive or even a complex one. There are no conditions – the outlaw can be brought in either dead or alive.

The desperate advertisement hints at a justice system that can't keep up: 'We're running out of ideas here – can you help?' The poster makes you tremble with hints of out-of-control lawlessness. And yet. All that money. Yours, if you back yourself.

Rewards for some of the most famous criminals were large in their context. Billy the Kid was worth US$500 in 1880;[3] Butch Cassidy was worth US$4000 in 1902;[4] and the reward for Jesse James rose steadily as he evaded capture, until it arrived at US$10,000 in 1882.[5]

There's a classic movie trope where fugitives are in a diner or something similar when breaking news comes over the TV. The police are disseminating their mugshots and warning the public. The dawning realisation on the face of the proprietor is a staple in any such scene – as is the screeching of tyres as the fugitives make their getaway. (If it's a Tarantino movie, intersperse a body-count in the dozens between the facial expression and the screeching tyres.)

In Chapter 2 – about price incentives – we met Goodhart's Law, which is about how the links between causes and effects that seem solid become ethereal when you use them for control. We also briefly met Goodhart's close cousin, the Lucas Critique. This critique, famous in the world of economics, posits that when you intervene in a system, everything you know about how people behave, the relationships you observed – the observations that guided your intervention – all change.

That scene in the diner is the Lucas Critique made concrete in a moment of high-adrenaline, high-consequence violence. Yes, someone probably has information that could lead to a simple arrest. Yes, it would be good if they knew the police needed that information. But the minute you put the criminal on a wanted poster – or on the TV or another medium – everything changes.

The unintended consequences of a reward for a criminal are not just the increased risk to those law-abiding citizen who encounter the outlaws. Outlaws also have a strong incentive to go on the run. This is the reason wanted posters have performed so amazingly badly over history at actually getting perpetrators caught.

Wanted posters bring us several lessons about the operation of incentives. Not only do wanted posters operate on the criminal, sharply reducing their willingness to be seen, but bounties aren't always paid when they are deserved, diminishing their reputation and usefulness. And the administrators of the justice system – the police themselves – can also be affected by bounties in ways that are not good for justice.

Wigs and badges

In a perfect world, we have enough police to do the job of crime fighting without involving volunteers. We keep all the crime-fighting incentives inside the police, where we can monitor performance, offer pay and promotions, and keep the unintended consequences on a tight leash.

But there is no perfect world. Rewards are still part of the mix in policing, especially in so-called 'cold cases' where collecting new information is hard.

Across history, places where rewards are most prominently offered are usually places a very long way from perfection. The archetype is the US frontier. The West was not only Wild in the natural sense, or in terms of behaviour. It was also a bureaucratic mess. Stuart Traub, whose work on bounty hunting in the late twentieth century is the leading scholarship in the area, writes this:

> *Lawlessness in the West was exacerbated by the absence of an effective system of law enforcement. In the late 1800s, territories were jurisdictionally controlled by US marshals, popularly elected sheriffs and constables with their deputies, local police forces, and Indian officers. At the very least, local, state and federal law enforcement was disorganised, erratic, contradictory and in many instances, politically motivated and arbitrary.*[6]

Funds for law enforcement were completely insufficient. Judges were untrained. Most towns lacked proper jails. There was lots of space to hide in, and posses were expensive to provision. Witnesses weren't compensated for travelling the often long distances to appear in court, so they didn't. Criminals often escaped or were found not guilty. What you had was a mess of many weak incentive systems. Rules overlapped and punishments weren't enforced.

To compensate for these weaknesses, as the frontier moved west-ward from Ohio to Utah during the nineteenth century, rewards began to pop up, generally in the range of $25 to $100. The US Government – desperate to prevent a rash of federal crimes, including mail robberies and forgeries – was the first to offer rewards. But it was a slow process, with the US attorney general having to sign off on every reward offered. Justice was rarely served.

Even if an associate knew a criminal's whereabouts, they would rarely sell them out. And if private citizens had information that could lead to an arrest they would generally offer that information anyway. Only rarely would a few hundred dollars be enough to make a person rat on his brother, or spend days riding around the wilderness looking for dangerous men. As an incentive in the justice system, rewards often failed because hunting for bad guys was costly (even without taking into account the chance of failure and the odds of turning up dead). The counter-incentives were stronger.

Deputy US Marshal JW Evans wrote to his superiors for funds in 1881. Cowboys had been committing crimes in Arizona, and, he argued, a posse of 200 men would need to be funded and equipped for 30 days at a cost of something close to US$30,000 in 1881 dollars.[7] As someone who has worked in the public service, I know an ambit claim when I see one. It's not recorded how much money he actually received.

The institutions with the money to offer substantial rewards were often not the officials but the businesses that spanned the west. Railroads and trading companies reached over far greater areas than any local law enforcement official – and their desire to apprehend criminals crossed state lines. Furthermore, the depth of their pockets gave them the capacity to offer rewards that caught the eye. When a US$5000 reward was put up for each member of the Dalton gang, the funds were put up by the Missouri, Kansas and Texas Railroad.[8]

In an era when labourer's wages were perhaps $1.50 a day, $5000 was serious money. However, chasing rewards was not a great occupation. If you believe Hollywood, the Wild West was crawling with bounty hunters, but, historians regretfully inform us, there were few or no real full-time professional bounty hunters. It just didn't pay. Rewards were intermittent and spread out over great distances. Those who collected them were often opportunistic locals getting a windfall. Like Bill Dunn, who had a fortuitous brush with two members of the Dalton gang.

On 2 May 1895, Bill Dunn and one of his brothers shot and killed Charley Pierce and Bitter Creek Newcomb, who had stabled their horses in the Dunn's barn. The bodies were taken to Guthrie Oklahoma and a $5000 reward was collected.[9]

This is another kind of case, where we can't be sure the reward did anything. Absent the reward, perhaps Bill Dunn would simply have alerted the sheriff that intruders were in his barn, saving two lives and $5000.

Rewards didn't always serve justice, and they sometimes had peculiar side effects. One of my favourite examples of an unexpected side effect comes from Louisiana in 1813. After a series of brazen crimes on the Gulf of Mexico, the governor of the state of Louisiana offered US$500 for capture of one Jean Lafitte, a French-born pirate. Lafitte was well known for smuggling all over the Gulf states and their waters. But no information was flushed out. Instead, shortly afterwards Lafitte (or an ally) put up posters all over New Orleans offering $500 for the capture of the governor. The Americans never laid their hands on Lafitte, who died years later in the Caribbean during a battle against the Spanish Navy.[10]

Scrutiny on the bounty

What made the bounty system even less reliable was its administration. Those who held the purse strings were powerful men, while the people coming in to claim were generally not. Rewards often went unpaid.

One of the most brazen examples of an unpaid reward is the story of Robert Ford. Ford infiltrated the infamous Jesse James gang and earned the trust of its leader. Jesse James was wanted dead or alive, and Ford was in touch with the authorities.

On 3 April 1882, Robert Ford shot Jesse James dead, handed himself in to the courthouse and contacted the police for his $10,000 reward. But Ford, who had shot James in the back of the head, soon got bad press. By the next day, the *St Louis Post-Dispatch* was referring to his actions as 'cold-blooded treachery', an accusation that presumably helped the justice system save $10,000.[11] Instead of being rewarded, Robert Ford was sentenced to hang and then, as a consolation, pardoned. Ford went free, but he never got his money.[12]

While citizens were being denied rewards, police were scooping them up. You may be surprised to hear that rewards could be collected by the police themselves. Well, they certainly could – and the police worked hard to get them. A voluntary organisation of police called the Rocky Mountain Detective Association distributed information on bandits and outlaws and made sure its members were paid if the bad guys were brought in.

Should law enforcement be allowed to collect rewards? One argument says no. While police are in search of convictions, bounty hunters can bring in bodies. There may be a double incentive for police in shooting first and asking questions later: they don't try the dead, and you never have to make a court appearance or compile evidence if you bring the person in dead instead of alive.

That's not the only way rewards could affect police behaviour. As police began to collect rewards, some were accused of waiting until rewards were posted before making arrests they could have made sooner. Would police really do that? By this stage of the book I hope you'd guess that yes, of course some would. Incentives are powerful enough to make at least some people forget their higher purpose some of the time.

That the bounty system – a simple incentive program – did little to further the administration of justice and indeed may have perverted justice is sadly not atypical of law enforcement, as we will see.

Forensic fallibility

When it comes to justice there are areas where dodgy incentives are easy to believe: we can easily see how drug squad police on the front line might easily be tempted. Other areas, less so. For example, forensics: we imagine a sterile and neutral domain in which truth is determined. But unfortunately, we have failed to hermetically seal the operating environment from infection by pernicious incentives. This is especially true in the US, where a dizzying array of failures has come to light thanks to some strong investigative journalism.

In February 2010, Greg Taylor was released from a prison in North Carolina – and his freedom tasted all the sweeter because not only was Taylor free, he was now declared innocent.

Taylor was overjoyed to see his daughter again:

She was nine years old when I went to prison ... I missed her tenth birthday, I missed her sixteenth birthday ... I missed her marriage. I missed the birth of my grandson. Now all of that's returned.[13]

In 1991 the body of a woman was discovered in a street in Raleigh, North Carolina. She had been beaten to death and Greg Taylor's truck was parked in the same street. When he showed up the next morning to get his truck, police arrested him. They found blood stains in the back of the truck, and Taylor was convicted of murder and jailed.

Taylor had his conviction overturned after the North Carolina Innocence Project took a look at his case. They made short work of it. The stains police found in his truck? That wasn't blood. A forensic laboratory had performed multiple tests on the marks at the time of Taylor's arrest and trial. The first one found 'chemical indication for the presence of blood'. Subsequent tests found it wasn't blood, but the legal teams – both prosecution and defence – never got to see the later reports.[14] The forensic lab knew what police wanted, and it wasn't an embarrassing reversal when a suspect was already on the hook.

Taylor's case was not unique. The same lab had done a similar thing in 230 other cases, withholding evidence that could lead to a finding of innocence while submitting evidence that could lead to a finding of guilt.[15]

As academics Roger Koppl and Meghan Sacks have written, 'Police, prosecutors, and forensic scientists often have an incentive to convict someone, with little or no incentive to convict the right someone.'[16]

A police officer with a high rate of convictions will look like a very effective officer. And when there are few mechanisms for reversing convictions, the downsides to convicting innocent parties are few. This incentive can flow through to forensic scientists when they work closely with police.

Koppl and Sacks bring forensic scientists into the group of people they believe can be perverted by the incentive to convict. In the last chapter we saw scientific principles turned to ash by the power of an incentive system. But when bad science is done in the forensic system, it's not only science but also justice that's ruined.

Koppl argues false conviction could be rampant and we would rarely find out. There are very few ways to judge the accuracy of criminal convictions; the system itself exists to provide a final determination, and that is normally that. An exception arises when a technical advance permits additional determinations to be done after a conviction is made. For example, when DNA evidence was first invented, it became possible to go back through cases from the preceding years and test the false conviction rate. One study that attempted this found the rate was a concerningly high 3 per cent.[17] That points to substantial and frightening failures in the justice system: for every 1000 people that are locked up, 30 of them could be innocent. This is a system that is supposed to ensure the innocent go free before it locks up the guilty. If the real false conviction rate is even a fraction that high, the system has a real problem, and in the US at least some of these problems lie with the incentives placed on forensic scientists.

TV has given us a false impression of how forensic science is done. *NCIS* has a particularly notable forensic officer (portrayed by the actor Pauley Perrette until 2018) who works as an integral part of the investigative team. Any idea why that might not be a great idea?

Outside the world of TV procedurals, law enforcement investigators are unavoidably biased. They have crime statistics goals to meet and they want to meet them. Cases need to be cleared. There is a risk that the forensic officer who works closely with police will become subject to these pressures and produce evidence that supports the case the police want to build.

The bad news is that in many places, forensic services are far from independent. For example in Victoria, where I live, there is an enormous Forensic Services Department within the police force. Forensic science is inside the police in some places and outside in others, but creating a separate organisation to do the science does not guarantee independence either – not when money flows.

One practice employed in the US deserves special mention. In certain states of the US, forensic lab funding comes from the courts. Courts levy fees that are sent to the labs if defendants are convicted, which means the labs are paid only when they help make a conviction. One former FBI laboratory tech put it like this: 'People say we're tainted for the prosecution. Hell, that's what we do! We get our evidence and present it for the prosecution.'[18]

Sometimes you need to state the obvious, so here goes: that is bad. Really bad.

Most of us, including most of us on juries, believe forensic science is above suspicion. DNA evidence in particular carries enormous weight. But forensic evidence is as susceptible to dodginess as all other evidence. It depends not only on having been collected properly, but also on subjective judgement.

Take fingerprints. In one brilliant study, a researcher showed pairs of fingerprints to five experts. These were pairs that they had previously identified as a match years earlier in other cases. The experts were experienced practitioners. They had been in the game on average 17 years each. But the second time around, four of the five delivered different identifications. 'No match,' said three of them. One other delivered a different assessment but was less confident – 'insufficient information', they said.[19] The trick the researchers pulled on these experts was to provide contextual information that would shape their decision: they were told ahead of their assessment that the pairs of prints were not a match.

The specifics of the non-match are themselves a pointer to how subjective and biased forensics can be. In this case, the fingerprint experts were told the prints were a particular pair that had been famously wrongly matched by the FBI in connection with the 2004 Madrid train bombings. In this true case, the FBI had provided a swift '100 per cent match' identification for Brandon Mayfield, a lawyer from Oregon.[20] Mayfield's prints were on file because he had once been in the US military, but he'd converted to Islam in the period prior to the bombings. The US Government locked him up for 14 days before European investigators pointed out that the fingerprints did not in fact match and sense prevailed.

The contextual information – 'expect to not find a match' – was enough to change the assessment of four out of five experts on fingerprints they had previously declared a match. This is important, because when police and forensic experts work closely together, contextual information may be frequently provided by police to crime labs, biasing their results.

Take this story of a police officer telling the forensic examiner what to expect about a weapon. 'We know this guy shot the victim and this is the gun he used,' the examiner was told. 'All we want you to do is confirm what we already know so we can get the scumbag off the street. We will wait. How quick can you do it?' The examiner gave them their instant identification. The suspect confessed and led the police to a second pistol, of the same calibre and model as the one tested, which tests demonstrated was the real murder weapon.[21]

Forensic failure shows up especially vividly in US data. Looking into forensics reveals it to be far more of a mess than you would expect. For example, in September 2008, 'the Detroit Police crime laboratory was shut down following a Michigan State Police audit that found a 10 percent error rate in ballistic evidence'.[22]

It's not just the US making a mess of forensics. One Australian case stands out in particular: the case of Farah Jama, a 22-year-old Somali man convicted of the rape of a 48-year-old woman at a Melbourne nightclub in 2006. The woman (who had been unconscious) never testified against him. No witnesses ever recalled seeing Jama at the nightclub's mature-aged singles night where the rape was alleged to have taken place. He steadfastly denied ever being there.

Farah Jama was released after 16 months in jail when prosecutors admitted he had never been at the scene. They did, however, acknowledge that his DNA had been processed in the same laboratory just 28 hours prior to the test on the alleged victim.[23]

There had been a terrible mistake.

The conviction was based not only on a mix-up in evidence. The incentives on the justice system to convict also played a part.

The justice system is one of the three big incentive systems that hold our society together, along with the economy and democracy. If it's corrupt, if it fails, who corrects it?

The answer is concerning. A lot of exonerations in the US are delivered by 'innocence projects', which are non-profit entities largely based in universities and run on the volunteer labour of undergraduate law students. One especially famous innocence project is in Mississippi. It's headed by a law professor and was established with funding from the author of bestsellers *The Firm* and *The Pelican Brief*, John Grisham. Kudos to Mr Grisham. He has helped get several innocent people out of jail and several guilty people in.

But any incentive system that relies on a generous author of top-quality airport novels to provide ad hoc checks and balances is one that is arguably not sufficiently interested in generating its own.

Neither are true crime podcasts the solution. Let us state a general principle: it is not enough to rely on citizen curiosity and/or fury to act as a balance on corrupted incentive systems. It's like relying on revolutions to change your dictator. You need built-in systems of checks and balances and oversight that keep the incentives operating as they were intended. Without that the incentive systems for justice can deteriorate to such an extent that they not only undermine the principles of the police and law courts but the very goals for which they stand. When that happens, a system risks turning the population against it.

The big picture

The principles in science and justice are generalisable to other organisations. Incentive systems in organisations and institutions tend to decay and meander until the guiding principles of those institutions are at risk. Whenever the administrator of an incentive scheme can also benefit from the scheme, the whole principle of the institution can be undermined.

The most important such institution we've not mentioned yet is democracy. Democracy is an incentive system – in theory, whoever has the best ideas gets elected, and if they implement those ideas well they might get re-elected. It's a powerfully simple incentive structure encouraging fair governance.

Elected officials who benefit from the system also influence the systems. They figure out ways to bend the incentive system to their benefit. Elected officials gerrymander the boundaries of their electoral district to make sure they can't lose. And they accept campaign finance contributions to pay for advertisements so they can be in the public eye incessantly. These factors – and others – affect outcomes of elections far more than we would hope for in a utopian scenario where the best candidate wins. Cynical citizens shrug and say that's how it is. But each shrug accelerates decay of the naive, idealistic vision that democracy represents.

Free markets are another major institution susceptible to decay. Free enterprise is an incentive system where in theory the businesses that sell the best products at the best prices grow the biggest.

Businesses benefit from stable democracies where free markets have legitimacy due to taxation, regulation and competition. But once businesses grow big enough they also have input to those systems. Their political power can erode taxation, regulation, competition and the legitimacy of free enterprise until people want to overthrow the whole system.

CEO pay is a clear example of the pattern. The huge salaries are an incentive system to make the company's top executive perform as well as they possibly can. But CEOs and their allies help set executive pay! Even if they hire remuneration consultants, or appoint a remuneration committee, the expectation is clear. The beneficiaries of the incentive are involved in the process of managing it.

The saying 'power corrupts' is ancient, but by taking an incentives perspective to the issue of power we can help see it afresh. Like rotating a map 180 degrees, a new perspective on a familiar problem can help us find relationships we never saw before.

But we haven't finished with outlaws just yet.

Chapter 12

Injustice, Armour and Fire

The year is 1878. A man is on the run. This man who is wanted so desperately did not hide out in Ohio, Kansas or in Wyoming. He was not pursued by a giant railway company nor the US Federal Government. The man with history's biggest price on his head was Edward 'Ned' Kelly, an Australian bushranger.

Ned Kelly was, in his own words, 'A widow's son and an Outlaw'.[1] He lived only 25 years, but his life has become Australia's most enduring myth. More has been written and said about him than any other Australian in history, and he is sewn deep into Australian culture. A book about him won the Booker Prize. He's been depicted in films by both Mick Jagger and Heath Ledger. Kelly is depicted in countless tacky souvenirs but also several priceless works of art hanging in the National Gallery. His story sustains a whole tourist industry and arguments continue to rage hot in the opinion pages over whether his memory should be celebrated at all.

As discussed in the last chapter, the justice system holds our fragile civilisation together. It prevents a potentially devastating eruption of violence and disorder. But the incentives of the justice system can be operated incorrectly and slide towards injustice.

If you run an incentive system capriciously, unreliably and in

185

an unjust fashion, you fail to reap the behaviours the incentives are supposed to create. This is a waste. But a failing incentive system can be worse than merely a waste. It can also encourage distrust in the institutions that run that incentive system, defiance of their authority, and – at the extreme – support of their opponents. An incentive system set up for good reasons can, if maladministered, end up fomenting opposition to its operators. If a democracy is corrupt, the people can turn against the allegedly 'elected' officials. And if a justice system is corrupt, criminals can begin to defy the police with support of the public.

Defiance can make some criminals into folk heroes. And on that note, we shall turn back to the man who deserved the biggest reward in history.

The reward on Ned Kelly's head was £8000, equivalent to over $US39,000 in 1878. That is almost four times the giant prize of US$10,000 offered for Jesse James. To think of it in terms of contemporary wages, the reward is close to A$4.5 million. The reward stayed the biggest in history, in inflation-adjusted terms, until the US Government put a US$25 million bounty on the head of Osama bin Laden.

The bin Laden reward, incidentally, was used in similar circumstances to that of the rewards of the Wild West. Bin Laden's hiding place (it turned out to be Pakistan) was poorly governed. There was very little in the way of police capacity there and even less American investigative capacity. What's more, the reward didn't work. Despite the poverty of the area in which bin Laden was hiding, the reward was never collected.

Kelly's reward was far more than an ordinary person could hope to make in a lifetime. And yet, of course, it didn't really work. As an enormous manhunt went on, Ned Kelly ranged free in the glorious Victorian bush for nearly two years.

The Kelly Gang

Victoria is the smallest of Australia's mainland states, tucked in the south-east corner. It punches far above its weight, however, being at the time of writing the second-most populous, and therefore the most densely populated mainland Australian state.

With its mountainous north-east, and grazing lands in the west, Victoria gives little of itself over to desert. The north-east is a particularly special part of the world. Eucalypts with proud bearing go straight up into bright blue skies. Rosellas fly fast like fighter jets between the tree trunks while cockatoos flock and create a ruckus.

The mountains on which those trees grow are ancient – this is not a new landscape brashly formed by the geological mashing of plates. The continent of Australia has been under a process of erosion for millions of years. But the erosion has not created benign Scottish fens or rolling hills; the mountains are rocky. Harsh. Kangaroos move through the grasslands in the valleys, and wallabies hop in and out of the ferns and bracken on the mountainside. In winter, snow. In summer, fires. This is the country in which Ned Kelly roamed free for years.

Ned Kelly was a paradox. Despite the natural human desire for justice and Kelly's brazen defiance of a justice system, he was the beneficiary of substantial popular support. He was a violent criminal and also a hero.

The reason those two things could co-exist? Victoria Police was a mess. The corruption of the nineteenth-century police force is the context in which Kelly must be understood. Kelly did not win sympathisers because people loved robbery and killing; it was because he personified rebellion against a police force widely agreed to be terrible.

Kelly's fame has many elements. His iconic armour is perhaps the most famous, with a helmet that obscured everything but his eyes. But another support for his centrality in Australian folklore is the Jerilderie Letter.

This letter, written in 1879, is a sprawling 8000-word memoir/ tirade/manifesto that contains many details of killings and many threats (also: almost no punctuation and yet almost no spelling errors). Its language is far more poetic than any bushranger should have the capacities to produce. It's also funny: 'Brooker Smith Superintendent of Police he knows as much about commanding Police as Captain Standing does about mustering mosquitoes and boiling them down for their fat.'

Kelly has no shortage of inventive insults: 'A parcel of big ugly fat necked wombat headed big bellied magpie legged narrow hipped splawfooted sons of Irish bailiffs or English landlords which is better known as Officers of Justice or Victorian Police.'

And Kelly has a keen eye for problematic incentives: 'it is a credit to a Policeman to convict an innocent man but any muff can pot a guilty one', he writes. The main reason to read it – and I recommend it to you – is for the portrayal of injustice. Its most dogged theme is a cry against a failing incentive scheme. Police corruption and brutality are at its core.

This is how Kelly writes of police visiting his mother's house.

They used to rush into the house upset all the milk dishes break tins of eggs empty the flour out of the bags on to the ground and even the meat out ... and destroy all the provisions and shove the girls in front of them into the rooms like dogs so as if any one was there they would shoot the girls first but they knew well I was not there or I would have scattered their blood and brains like rain I would manure the Eleven mile with their bloated carcases.

The Jerilderie letter is full of blood and gore. This Australian hero was a violent man. And yet he is lionised. Why?

He fits into that narrow band of criminals whose exploits satisfy our sense of justice. He is like Robin Hood robbing from the rich of Nottingham, old-world pirates plundering from the world's most powerful navies, or Omar from *The Wire* robbing murderous drug dealers. Some criminals – when they target a powerful and unjust authority and defy them long enough – ascend to another level.

If criminals can become folk heroes by defying the law, it suggests the authority of the law has become as illegitimate as the authority wielded by the drug dealers in *The Wire*.

This is how risky it is to try to achieve even very legitimate goals through administering incentives. The incentive might work in theory. But in practice its operators can let it down; they can make a decent system cruel and unfair. The risk is especially acute for punishments. If we let the administration of punishments decay and slip into corruption, the people on whom these incentives are inflicted may be able to rouse substantial public sympathy, and the original noble ideals the incentives were designed to support may be forgotten in a maelstrom of anger about how they were applied in practice.

Poorly administered punishment systems risk undermining the very purpose of the institutions that glue our civilisation together. Whether we work in government or act as citizens, we must oppose those who tolerate the bending of the rules. Exemptions from the rules, it is worth remembering, have a horrible way of creating precedents. Being unsmiling and grave in monitoring incentives is especially vital when it comes to the police.

So should we celebrate someone like Ned Kelly, who stands up against the police? I say yes, but only if we remember why. Not all power is benign. Defying the cruel or unfair use of power can create a push for justice.

'Marred by favouritism, ill-considered decisions and corruption'²

What keeps corruption out? Who watches the watchers? This is one of the key problems of any incentive system that's large enough. It's an acute problem with policing.

In 2018, while I was writing this book, police corruption regularly made front-page news. The incentives on police to convict the innocent, let the guilty go free, take money from crime scenes, pervert justice, use defence lawyers as snitches and generally deploy their extensive powers for their own nefarious purposes are very resilient. (All this in the Australian state of Victoria, which has been described as 'Australia's Massachusetts'. It's perhaps the most moderate and sedate state in one of the world's most modern and well-functioning democracies. If we have problems here it shows just how hard it must be to completely eradicate corruption in a police force.)

If corruption is troubling now, it was even worse in the nineteenth century, when Victoria Police lacked oversight almost completely. They were outrageously, even comically bad.

Let's go back to the beginning. In 1836, the year after Melbourne's founding, the growing settlement first needed police. A request was dispatched and three officers were sent down from the established colony of Sydney. All three were surplus to requirements in New South Wales, and it turned out that was because they had been dismissed for drunkenness. Their new postings failed to cure them of that predilection. We were off to a very bad start. Two of the next recruits were former convicts, and they also lasted only for short stints. This run of awful luck continued – in 1838 the chief constable of Melbourne City Police was dismissed for bribery.

In 1851 Victoria was established as a separate colony from New South Wales. In 1852 it got its own official police force. In that same year, the Select Committee on Police heard 'there has been, in the case of several detective officers, a most suspicious suddenness in getting rich'.[3] By 1854 Victoria Police needed to construct a special prison just to hold *police officers* who had broken the law.[4]

Victoria Police, in short, ran amok. Police heavy-handedness was largely responsible for the 1854 Eureka Stockade, Australia's very own revolution, where goldminers, soldiers and police fought to the death. (A revolutionary movement can be born by the unjust operation of an incentive scheme. This is an idea we'll return to later.)

Law enforcement did not have to be this way, even then. As we know, a good system of rules, punishments and payoffs can help modify any kind of behaviour. But there was no such system in place to control the behaviour of Victoria Police. Officers were low-paid and untrained, poorly supervised and deemed the least valuable of all civil servants in the colony. Furthermore, problems with Victoria Police behaviour started at the top.

For most of Ned Kelly's life, the Commissioner of Police was a gentleman named Frederick Standish. He led the force from 1858 to 1880, if 'led' is the right word. An official police source describes Standish like this:

> *His easygoing and luxurious lifestyle impaired both the public image and the internal morale of the Force. Moreover, his stewardship as Chief Commissioner was marred by instances of favouritism, ill-considered decisions and corruption.*[5]

A major, independent public inquiry into the failures of Victoria Police during the hunt for the Ned Kelly argued the same. Standish was a terrible leader and the Victoria Police was rotting away under him. This finding was the result of the most serious and powerful kind of public enquiry available in Australia, known as a royal commission. A separate royal commission into the police just a few years later described a state of affairs that was possibly even worse, describing the Victoria Police Detective Force as 'a standing menace to the community'.[6]

We're not talking about a professionalised and well-compensated force like you find today (which is still very much capable of ongoing systemic corruption, but nevertheless respected by wider society). Amid the corruption and decay of nineteenth-century law enforcement, the utopian vision of a law-abiding society was so undermined that people who believed in justice were driven to support the opponents of the police. Ned Kelly had supporters almost everywhere.

The Kelly family

Both Ned's parents came from an Ireland ruled by the British. Ireland was extremely poor and before long British misrule would be a major cause of the Great Famine that killed a million people.

His father, John Kelly, was a convict with a bad reputation and his mother, Ellen Quinn, was an assisted migrant but a wild child who had resented school. When Ellen met John Kelly, they completed that classic two-step: pregnancy, followed by marriage.

Over a tumultuous 15 years from 1851, John and Ellen would have eight children, of which seven survived. Ned was born in 1855. In that period John Kelly got rich on the goldfields and was able to buy farmland of his own.

But neither land nor children could calm John Kelly. He stole, drank, went to jail and finally, aged 46, died of oedema. At his father's funeral, Ned Kelly was just 11 years old. With seven children, a farm less fertile than hoped, and the police ever vigilant (the broader Kelly and Quinn families were high on the Victoria Police radar), Ellen Kelly took off. Exiled among exiles, she took her seven children and set out for the parts of Australia into which the fewest Europeans had trod.

Moving away from town could not stop the inevitable. Ned Kelly was put in jail for the first time – a six-month sentence he considered very unfair – aged about 15. The crimes of Ned Kelly were mostly limited to fighting, drunkenness, cattle rustling and horse thievery – until 1878.

In that year a single policeman caused a major turning point. A constable called Fitzpatrick – who had been at the pub drinking – called in at the Kelly home to arrest Ned's brother Dan. A ruckus ensued, and Fitzpatrick claimed Ned Kelly had shot him in the wrist then extracted the bullet with a knife. The alternative story is that Ned was not there and Fitzpatrick injured his wrist in a scuffle.[7]

Ned's mother and two other men were charged with aiding and abetting the attempted murder of Constable Fitzpatrick. They were tried in Beechworth before Justice Redmond Barry, and despite the uncertainty of Fitzpatrick's evidence, Barry convicted them. With their mother in custody, Ned and his brother Dan took off into the bush. But the police were in pursuit.

Stringybark

On 26 October 1878, Ned Kelly, age 24, killed a man for the first time. A party of four police searching for the Kellys had set up camp at Stringybark Creek. They were unsubtle, drawing attention to their location by shooting at birds. The police did not have to wait long before Ned Kelly and his brother, along with friends Joe Byrne and Steve Hart, surrounded their camp.

Two policemen were killed in a shoot-out on the scene and one was apparently murdered a short distance away, after being injured.

The fourth constable – Thomas McIntyre, who had at first surrendered meekly – escaped.

Three policemen were dead. The band of men responsible was now known as the 'Kelly Gang', deemed a significant threat to law and order in the colony of Victoria.

Within weeks of the Stringybark murders, the Felon's Apprehension Act introduced the concept of outlawry into Victorian law. (Australia was not a single entity until 1901, when the various colonies joined together to become a single country. New Zealand had been in the running to join too but, in the end, they wisely kept a safe distance. So at the time there was no Australian law; each colony had its own.)

Under the new Victorian law, to capture a felon, you could use force from the outset. As summarised by MP Dr John Madden:

> If any person were to venture to shoot one of these men whose lives are now forfeit under the law, without previously calling upon him to surrender, that person would be liable to be placed on his trial for murder, and probably he would be convicted of manslaughter ...
>
> But under this Bill a person may stalk them; he may steal upon them, and shoot them down as he would shoot a kangaroo. Under the law as it stands, for doing that, he would be liable to be tried for murder.[8]

(Dr Madden is trying to support the legislation with these comments.)

The Felon's Apprehension Act was a piece of legislation that betrayed little understanding of how its incentives would work. An outlaw is someone who, by ignoring the law, no longer has the protection of the law. They are fair game – can be taken dead or alive. The Kellys, who had a known address and frequented the towns of north-east Victoria, responded to the new incentives by sinking into the bush.

Bushrangers already used the protection of the dense Australian bush to help them commit crimes, but with a law like this hanging over their heads, they would go even deeper. The idea that citizens would have regular opportunities to kill these outlaws no longer held true. The Kelly Gang were rarely seen, and when they came into towns they did so swiftly and secretly.

The Kelly Gang came to the town of Euroa to rob the bank in December 1878. It was a stealth operation. They were careful to operate in utmost secrecy, surprising all the people who saw them and taking all comers hostage, so none could raise the alarm. The gang slunk back into the bush carrying thousands of pounds of gold and cash.

Their 8 February 1879 spree at Jerilderie was a bit more reckless – they even drank in the hotels – but Jerilderie was in New South Wales and they could perhaps pass unrecognised. The gang robbed the Jerilderie bank of around £2000, burned mortgage documents held at the bank, and also took all the police horses so they could not be pursued. It was in Jerilderie that Kelly handed over to a bank employee his autobiography/manifesto, the aforementioned Jerilderie Letter.

As the Kelly Gang hid out in the bush, the authorities tried to figure out how to capture them. Letters to the editor of major newspapers poured in, offering free advice to the government.

'The capture of the Kellys should be regarded as a matter of money', advised one letter published in *The Argus* on 14 February 1879. It suggested a reward of £8000 and a free pardon plus exit from the colony for any accomplice or informer.[9]

The police did raise the reward, and I do not pretend the reward had no effect on society. Many wanted it. But very few had any chance of getting close to Ned Kelly. Furthermore, in a particularly savage demonstration of the Lucas Critique – the idea that intervening in a system changes it in ways that you never foresaw – the Kelly Gang set up their own incentive system. Theirs was designed to directly neutralise the enormous reward, and it didn't require thousands of pounds: it ran on fear. By killing one informant they could silence many more.

The last stand

The police worked hard to find informers that could lead them to the Kelly Gang. Police records preserve many letters from odd-bods writing in and offering their services. Most of them were incredible long shots and therefore ignored.

But the police had one man who might actually help: Aaron Sherritt. Sherritt had gone to both school and prison with Kelly Gang member Joe Byrne and was an associate of the Kelly brothers. They had even engaged in a bit of horse stealing together (allegedly). But in 1879 a witness testified in court that Aaron Sherritt had been seen with 'police horses in his paddock'.[10] The implication was he was working with the police.

How long the Kelly Gang suspected Sherritt is not known. But on the evening of 26 June 1880, they took action.

Joe Byrne and Dan Kelly captured one of Sherritt's neighbours, a market gardener by the name of Antoine Weekes, and took him to Sherritt's front door to entice Sherritt out. Weekes later testified at a magisterial enquiry that he knocked on Sherritt's door and claimed that he was lost (an odd thing for a neighbour to say, really).

But Sherritt was not suspicious enough and came to speak with Weekes. As Sherritt emerged, Byrne shot him. Then, according to the hostage, Byrne approached the hut, '… looked into the place and said "That's all; that is the man I want."'[11]

After Sherritt was killed Dan Kelly and Joe Byrne remained outside the hut for a short period, apparently trying to burn it down. Sherritt was concealing four police constables in his hut that night – history does not record if they were there to get information, or for Sherritt's protection. (If the latter, they failed miserably.) The policemen hid in the bedroom overnight, emerging only at dawn, hours after the two outlaws had departed.

Later, in court proceedings, the jury laughed at this last piece of testimony.[12] The image of four armed policemen hiding under a bed long after the Kellys had gone fitted perfectly into a narrative the public already believed – the police were ineffective, gutless and terrified of the powerful Kelly Gang.

The Kelly Gang's reputation for retribution would have been heightened by the killing of an informer under strong police guard. Such an act would likely have bought them protection from informants for some time. But it turned out they didn't have much time left; within days the gang had their last stand.

The siege of Glenrowan is a story that has been told many times. It was here that Ned Kelly most famously donned his iconic steel armour – made from old ploughs – and was able to survive a barrage of oncoming fire. Historians have written volume upon volume about it, so we won't go into all the detail. The part of this tale most relevant to our topic is the behaviour of one Thomas Curnow.

Curnow, a schoolteacher, was one of the 60-something hostages the Kelly Gang imprisoned in the Glenrowan Hotel. The gang had locked up most of the town while they waited for a train to round a corner and hit a section of track they had destroyed. The train was chosen carefully. It was a 'special' full of police bound for Beechworth, in response to the murder of Aaron Sherritt. The train was intended to derail above a steep embankment and tumble down it.

Curnow managed to trick Ned Kelly into releasing him by suggesting he was a sympathiser and promising he would not tell anyone what was happening. But instead of keeping his promise, Curnow went to the train line and flagged down the train before it could derail.

According to the Longmore Commission, 'to [Curnow's] tact, coolness, and bravery, must be attributed the rescue of the special train and its occupants from destruction'.[13]

The Kelly Gang had made a strategic blunder. Everything rested on the train derailing. Now, instead of them going after the police from a position of advantage, the roles were reversed.

Before long the Glenrowan Hotel – still filled with hostages as well as the gang members themselves – was surrounded.

The police fired heavily on the small weatherboard hotel, killing some of the hostages. And they also sent for the big guns. Literally. Superintendent Hare, the most senior officer on the scene, contacted Melbourne to request a cannon. Victoria Police command found one and put it on the first train north.[14]

Waiting several hours for the cannon evidently grew wearisome because before it arrived the police changed course and set fire to the hotel instead (by now we won't be shocked by any of their tactical decisions). By that time most of the hostages had been killed or released, but not all.

Aghast at what he was witnessing, a local clergyman ran into the burning hotel. He brought out one hostage, who died shortly after, and the body of Joe Byrne. The clergyman said he had seen the bodies of Dan Kelly and Steve Hart, killed in a suicide pact or perhaps by police bullets.[15] Their bodies were destroyed by the flames.

Only Ned Kelly survived the siege, leaving the hotel and circling round to flank the police. Here's how *The New York Times* described what happened:

Ned Kelly, the leader, left the hotel during the fight and returned in the morning. It was nearly 8 o'clock when his tall figure was seen close behind the line of police. His head, chest, back and sides were all protected with heavy plates of quarter-inch iron. When within easy distance of Senior Constable Kelly, who was watching him, he fired. The Police then knew who he was and fired on the ruffian. The contest became one which from its remarkable nature almost baffles description. Nine policemen joined in the conflict and fired point blank at Kelly, but although it was apparent that many of the shots struck him, in consequence of the way in which he staggered, yet he always recovered himself, and, tapping his breast, laughed derisively at his opponents as he coolly returned their fire, fighting only with a revolver.[16]

Kelly's thick armour repelled incoming fire until the police realised it didn't extend below the thigh. Once he was shot a couple of times in the leg, Kelly was forced to surrender. He was arrested and imprisoned in Melbourne.

Ultimately Kelly could not outrun the law. He was tried, found guilty and hanged.

You can only imagine what might have happened to perceptions of functioning authority had Thomas Curnow not prevented the train from derailing. The reward for Ned Kelly might have grown even larger and the official hunt would surely have redoubled. Government powers might have been increased and police given extra resources, which no doubt would have further inspired opposition to them. The whole history of Victoria might have taken on a rather more authoritarian bent.

Following the siege at Glenrowan, the giant reward was finally dispersed. Did it go entirely to the heroic Thomas Curnow? No.

The single biggest recipient of the reward was a policeman. £800 was given to the man who had been leading the unsuccessful hunt for the Kellys over the preceding period, Police Superintendent Francis Hare.

Every other policeman who was in Glenrowan that day was also rewarded. Three dozen constables received sums between £42 and £275, with 80 per cent of the reward going to police. The exceptions were the police trackers who had travelled down from Queensland for the manhunt. They were allocated £50 each in the official division of monies but the sum was never paid, as Indigenous people were not deemed full members of society (their payments were given to the Queensland and Victoria governments to be 'dealt with at their discretion').

In total the reward was officially allocated to over 60 people, including senior constables, sergeants, superintendents, a detective and a few railway personnel who had been aboard the train. Thomas Curnow received just under 7 per cent of the award, or £550.[17] I only wish we could see what Ned Kelly would have written had he heard about that.

Victorians were hardly shocked that the rewards went mostly to the police themselves. Nor were they perturbed that the Queensland trackers had been denied anything. But the puny payment to the heroic Curnow was enough to provoke dissent. As reported in the Brisbane *Telegraph*,

> Complaint was made that Mr. Thomas Curnow had not been allotted a sufficient sum … further inquiry has produced the general conviction that Mr Curnow should be more liberally dealt with. It is recognised that when civilians generally were standing aloof, in a cautious, if not a cowardly, spirit, Mr. Curnow risked his life to aid the police, and was the means of averting a possible terrible calamity. But for him the pilot engine would have been hurled into the cutting, as the Kellys anticipated, and the special train might have gone after it.[18]

Did the reward work? Curnow later said he didn't act because of the incentive but out of a sense of duty.[19] Of course a person is hardly likely to admit venal aims to themselves, let alone announce them to the world. So we cannot be certain. Perhaps the outsize reward did inspire an extra level of bravery in Curnow. We can never be entirely sure if those wanted posters did anything to bring Ned Kelly down.

What we know is that the last 140 years have seen big innovations in creating incentives to drive good behaviour by police. Corruption has been dramatically reduced and professionalism has risen sharply. Hong Kong in particular is famous for turning a bent police force into a straight one. So what are the systems that have worked?

Part of the answer has been higher pay and more training. Underpaid and under-trained police are far more likely to respond to every little tempting incentive that comes their way, whether that is accepting bribes to let criminal activity run, or misusing their authority to crack down on good citizens. Police who intend to make an entire career out of being a police officer and who can expect a good living from it will be less tempted to break the rules.

That's not enough though. It's important police actually perceive their career to be at risk if they do break the rules. So the second big change is in increasing the perceived likelihood of punishment for bad behaviour.

Bad police have always been subject to discipline and demotion; the problem was they were so easily able to deny the misbehaviour and evade discipline. Police interviews are now usually videotaped, and closed-circuit cameras run in police stations. These go a long way to reducing the freedom some police feel they have to break the rules. They also help break down the culture of covering up for colleagues. If you lie about what another police officer did and the video later shows him bashing the suspect, you both go down. Technology changes incentives.

Police body cameras are a natural extension of this concept and have been adopted in some US jurisdictions. Random passers-by with smartphones are also providing evidence of police misbehaviour. All of these monitoring systems make the administration of consequences far more straightforward, as they make it much easier to prove misbehaviour.

A final piece of the reform of police incentives is external independent organisations that have strong powers to control corruption. The original and most often emulated of these is Hong Kong's Independent Commission Against Corruption. It transformed the Hong Kong Police from a mess of bribery and corruption to a beacon of good practice within a few decades.[20]

'The Whole of Hong Kong operates on a commission basis,' wrote Justice Alastair Blair-Kerr in 1973. Corruption was widespread and most entrenched in the police. For the 20 years between 1953 and that statement, there were more reports of police corruption than in all other government departments combined. But in 1973, after the so-called 'Godber incident' – in which a senior policeman named Godber collected hundreds of thousands of dollars in corrupt payments and eluded a warrant for his arrest by making off to Britain – the issue reached a fever pitch. ICAC was established and came out guns blazing. It prosecuted hundreds of corrupt officials in its first few years. Police did not like it and threatened to strike, but ICAC carried on and results began to show. In a regular survey, the share of citizens who believed that corruption was present in most government departments fell from 38 per cent in 1977 to 1 per cent in 2002.[21]

Similar bodies have been established all over the world. The New South Wales institution overseeing the police even shares a name with its Hong Kong progenitor. These bodies are powerful tools for applying oversight to otherwise untouchable agencies, but of course even an independent commission must be overseen. There are no limits on the recursion here. For corruption to be rooted out we must have watchers watching the watchers at every level, and above it all, a functioning democracy that can be regularly refreshed with idealistic reformers.

If we want incentives to work for us and not against us, we must be ever alert against decay and keep them aligned tightly with the original ideals they were designed to support.

Interlude

The Hunger Games

Warning: spoilers ahead.

One of the best recent pieces of work about incentives is, believe it or not, *The Hunger Games*. Not so much book one; from an incentives perspective, book one doesn't really stack up. Book two is where the magic happens.

The Hunger Games, if you are unfamiliar with it, is a trilogy of young adult science fiction novels written by Suzanne Collins. It follows a young person from an impoverished district of a fictional world forced into an incentive system: a gladiatorial battle to the death with 24 other children. These titular Hunger Games are held in an artificial arena of perpetually shrinking size, meaning combatants have no option but to face their competitors. And it's all broadcast for the amusement of citizens from the wealthy districts. (Put like that it sounds brutal and tasteless, but these books have sold millions of copies to young people around the world, and they appear to be turning out all right.)

Our hero, Katniss Everdeen, is a Legolas/Robin Hood type – very handy with a bow and arrow. Katniss prevails against the other children thanks to her amazing skills and essential goodness: she kills only a *few* of the other contestants, and she also saves the life of one contestant – so, you know, we don't hate her.

The Hunger Games can be read as a critique of colonialism, or, if you really want to go crazy, as a critique of contemporary market economic relations, where one group of poorer people (developing countries) are relied on to make things so that another class of richer people (the first world) is able to engage in more consumption.

The Hunger Games book one is fun, but it has a payoff structure that makes no sense. One of the key conceits of book one is that some young people *choose* to enter the Hunger Games and therefore face a very strong chance of death: 23 in 24, to be precise. These self-nominated competitors are called 'careers'. There are six careers in the arena in book one. Even if one of these six is the eventual winner, and not the other 18, the careers still face an 82 per cent chance of death. That must be concerning.

In the story, those children who elect to join the games are motivated by the prospect of the prize: lifelong food and housing. This kind of makes sense based on the fact that most of the competitors come from poor districts. But then we are told that the careers come from 'wealthier districts … fed and housed throughout their lives for this moment'.[1] It is hard to believe that a person from a wealthier district would forfeit their life in this way, and even harder to believe that their community would support and sanction their choice by investing resources in a project that has no community returns.

We can conclude that either these children (and their communities) place an exceedingly low value on their lives, or they place an unusually high value on lifelong free food and housing. (An alternative hypothesis is that the careers are the bad kids everyone wants to be rid of. This actually makes the most sense given what we learn about their characters in the book.)

The Hunger Games would be more grittily realistic if it were the children from the poorest districts who trained hard and entered the games deliberately. In real life, the sad truth is dangerous work and desperate choices tend to be the domain of people with the fewest alternatives.

Anyway, enough about book one. I want to talk about book two. Because in book two, we learn one of the most important lessons of incentive systems: you don't always have to accept them as they are.

The Hunger Games demonstrates the kind of incentive system we're all familiar with – one imposed on us by external forces we are powerless to resist. Children find themselves in this situation all the time, so the book is tremendously salient to them. But even as adults we are at the mercy of governments, market systems and corporate rules which are very hard – or even totally impossible – to opt out of. Whether you are being oppressed by your teachers or by capitalism, book two of *The Hunger Games* is for you.

In book two, Katniss Everdeen is sent back into the arena for another round of combat. Winners are not supposed to be sent back to the Hunger Games, so this move makes it clear that the rules are flexible – that they are a human construct and need not last forever. This plants the seeds for what happens next.

Katniss and several other contestants band together. Using wire, electricity and Katniss's archery skills, they manage to destroy the arena. The Hunger Games are over and the children escape.

Control over an incentive system is power. It is power that Katniss Everdeen and her friends win when they destroy the arena in which their lives were meant to end. Rather than taking an incentive structure as given, these young people dismantle it, refusing to accept a set of rules, payoffs and punishments, and replacing it with another. Suzanne Collins has just given a taste of revolution to millions of impressionable young minds.

'You say you want a ...'

Revolution is one way in which incentive systems end. A set of rules or a set of systems of rules disappoints enough people badly enough that they can be overthrown. They become evolutionarily 'unfit' and they exist no longer.

Revolution is also a powerful mechanism in the evolution of

'fit' systems. In any revolution, the system that is overthrown must be replaced by one that appeals to the newly powerful. Revolution can instil incentive systems that suit a great mass of people, like the democratic revolution in the former Czechoslovakia in 1989 or the independence movements in Kosovo and South Sudan.

But of course it is not always so simple. A military revolution can lead to concentration of power, and even popular revolution can sometimes lead to incentive systems that suit only some people – like the nationalisation of private property, the installation of a theocracy, or the demolition of a price incentive system. The history of the twentieth century was shaped by exactly these kinds of revolutions (in Cuba, Iran and the USSR, for example).

The twenty-first century has begun with revolutions that are less economic and more about freedom: the so-called colour revolutions in the former Soviet Union, and the Arab Spring uprisings across the Middle East. Not all have been successful.

The process of revolution is not as trivial as it is made out to be in a children's book – especially not the overthrow of a nation state. The worst nation states are often propped up by intrusive and harsh law enforcement. The desire to revolt increases unrest, which in turn increases the intrusion and harshness with which laws are applied.

These incentive systems are held in place only by power they themselves create. At this point fitness of the incentive system will no longer be determined by its appeal to the population but by its ability to keep the powerful in power. These are incentive systems that have decayed beyond repair – ripe for revolution.

It can be hard to pick that ripe fruit. A very unfriendly set of incentive systems can remain 'fit' enough to survive for a long time – in *1984* George Orwell writes of a boot stamping on a human face 'forever'. But so far no nation has lasted forever without changing. There is always hope.

Threat of revolution is one check on decay – preventing bad governments from becoming utter kleptocracies. China's opening to the world and adoption of market systems can be seen as such a pre-emptive move, granting the ruling Communist Party legitimacy and – it must hope – decreasing the chance of its system being dismantled.

A fresh start

In most parts of the affluent west, revolution feels like a topic for history. Our democratic systems may be operating with sand in their gears but they still clunk along.

The twenty-first century also offers far less opportunity for making dramatic new starts. A few centuries hence, one alternative to revolution was to board a boat and slip off to start a new country. The pilgrims did it, establishing an invigorating experiment in new incentive systems that would eventually become known as the United States of America.

This trick cannot be repeated. With the rights of indigenous peoples now rightfully recognised, the world's maps entirely drawn and Westphalian sovereignty completely hegemonic, starting new countries is bloody difficult. Of course there is the fringe movement of 'seasteading', which hopes to establish floating platforms or 'seasteads' that can operate as their own liberated societies, but this has had no success in any practical sense.

The more realistic twenty-first-century alternative to boarding a boat to start a new country is boarding a boat to join an existing country. Migration is a way in which good incentive systems prove both evolutionarily fit while also showing they are human-friendly. They gain adherents and so expand their reach. A refugee journey is not easy – it can involve a chance of death – but in a world of oppressive incentive systems, it is one way to escape. When we accept refugees, we extend the advantages of good systems to more people.

It is fitting that book two of *The Hunger Games* finishes with Katniss Everdeen on an aircraft, migrating away from the regime that has tortured her. (Although she comes back – with a vengeance – in book three, but that's a story for another day.)

Chapter 13

Climate Change

In 2018, I visited the Great Barrier Reef. It was one of the best days of my life.

I admit to bias. I love Australia and I love the ocean, so a day exploring an iconic Australian oceanic feature is my kind of day. We travelled out there on a big, slow boat that provided bottomless coffee. The weather was calm; the waves were small; it was delightful.

I was eager to visit the reef sooner rather than later because coral bleaching events are becoming more and more common. The reef will not be with us forever if the world's average temperature keeps rising, and scientists are increasingly confident that this is going to happen. Global warming – you might've heard of it. Human activity is releasing into the atmosphere particles that trap energy on Earth and cause average global temperatures to rise. These particles are mostly released by combustion reactions: burning things that are made of organic molecules rich in carbon, like coal and oil. Unfortunately this underpins our whole contemporary economy.

Changing temperatures are bad for many species, but coral is particularly affected because it is not mobile – it can't migrate to a new area. While the Great Barrier Reef will probably slowly extend itself southward as the world's oceans get warmer, it won't be nearly enough to make up for the large amounts of coral dying in its north.

When I visited the reef I went to a little island called Michaelmas Cay. A tiny lump of sand at the edge of a big coral formation, the cay has approximately 15 blades of grass growing on its very centre and provides home base for around one thousand sea birds.

We got off the boat and onto the beach, donned flippers and snorkels, and waded into the beautiful pale-blue waters of tropical north Queensland. We saw stingrays and parrot fish and spent a bit of time tracking down that elusive little guy, Nemo (i.e. the clownfish). I was particularly happy to see the sea turtles. It might sound simple but I find looking at animals awfully pleasing. (I suspect I am not alone. If the internet's crescendo of cat videos has taught us anything it is that our appetite for cute and surprising animals to look at went desperately unmet for years.)

The reef was teeming with interesting creatures. At that latitude, at that time of year, it was bright and full of life. We saw little bleaching. But future generations won't necessarily be able to say the same thing.

A speck of science

The idea of pollution is centuries old. One of the earliest recorded examples in the western world was London air quality – the first law against burning certain types of coal in the city was enacted by royal proclamation in 1307.[1] As the number of people in the world increases and the global economy doubles and redoubles, so the residue of our economic activity also increases. This residue is visible in many places. I see it whenever the river near my house bursts its banks and then recedes, the banks covered in plastic bottles and bags.

Rolling clouds of black smoke from coal burning or rivers filled with plastic are easy to see. But pollution is also lurking in places where it is less apparent. One of the places we were slowest to look for evidence of pollution was in the atmosphere. Unfortunately scientists now believe the atmosphere is where one of the most important side effects of human activity is found. Greenhouse gases floating around up there in the atmosphere have a small but powerful effect.

When energy from the sun travels to the earth, it does so at a wavelength that means it cannot be absorbed by greenhouse gases. But after it bounces *off* the earth's surface, the wavelength changes, and the energy of these wavelengths is absorbed by certain molecules in the atmosphere. This process is why our planet has a lovely warm temperature at all: these wavelengths make our planet habitable. But like all things, energy absorption is best in moderation. The more of those molecules that are up there, the higher the absorption. In the past, energy would easily bounce off the surface of the planet and back into the large heat sink we call outer space. These days more of it is trapped in our atmosphere.

Now to really get scientific. As this next equation shows, when you burn a fuel made of carbon (C) and hydrogen (H), it mixes with oxygen and the result is water and carbon dioxide.

$$CH + O_2 = H_2O + CO_2$$

Unfortunately all our favourite fuels – petrol, natural gas, kerosene, butane, coal – are made of hydrogen and carbon. When we dig them up and burn them, we add extra carbon dioxide to the atmosphere. At the time of writing, carbon dioxide concentrations in the atmosphere are at 410 parts per million – 45 per cent higher than when King Edward first grew cross at the effect of coal burning, and 20 per cent higher than in 1980 – and accelerating.[2] The timing of this leap in the carbon dioxide concentration of the atmosphere matches the adoption of modern middle-class lifestyles across the world, with all the energy use that entails.

While we mostly worry about carbon dioxide, there are also methane, ozone and other accumulating greenhouse gases emitted by other kinds of increasing human activity – for example farming animals. And these greenhouse gases last a long time before they break down.

The process by which gases trap heat is the 'greenhouse effect' (a term I certainly used to hear a lot in my childhood but which seems to have gone the way of Cabbage Patch Kids). Greenhouses actually work differently from the greenhouse effect, simply by trapping warm air, but this erroneously named effect is why since the 1880s things have been, on average, heating up.

By now a majority of people believe the climate change is real, so I won't recap all the facts for you – just know that the temperature in 2018 was around 1.5 degree Celsius higher than it was in the years 1951–1980.[3] However, there is a reason we don't call it global warming anymore. Temperature changes are not evenly spread out across the world: in some places the weather seem very much as normal; in other parts there have been dramatic shifts. Hence, climate change.

One of the areas that has seen the most pronounced change is one where very few people live – the Arctic Circle. Above 60 degrees of latitude, the temperature anomaly is twice the global average.[4] You have probably seen the videos of scrawny polar bears struggling onto ice floes that look about as thick and stable as a floating doormat. These are not the good type of animal internet videos. They are shocking to see.

I mean, sure, there are upsides. A mild arctic is great news for shipping: less ice means more access from America to Asia. No need to use the Panama Canal if you can just go over the top of the globe. Think of the savings on tolls!

But realistically this is dire news. Less ice means a darker surface of the earth and even more heat energy absorbed rather than reflected, exacerbating the warming effect.

Melting arctic sea ice would not cause dramatic rising sea levels. Arctic sea ice is relatively thin and mostly already in the sea anyway. It partially melts and re-freezes each year without budging sea levels much, so even though the ice extent keeps receding, we do not need to fear that it all melting will mean we all drown.

But there is an awful lot of permanent ice on nearby Greenland that has begun melting faster than before. That's a much bigger risk. If Greenland's ice-cover warms up and melts into the sea, high tides will start getting a lot higher. High enough to make waterfront property a liability rather than an asset – and I'm not just talking about a few beach houses.

Globally, many of those with the least resources to adapt to climate change live near the water. The sea is a source of sustenance to countless fishing communities. Whole Pacific nations lie just above sea level, and millions of people live in low-lying river deltas, especially in Bangladesh. Estimates of population displacement in Bangladesh alone are as high as 50 million people by 2100.[5]

The side effects of the operation of the coal and oil industries are becoming hazardous to life on earth. Species could be wiped out. *Homo sapiens* is not at any real existential risk – we are famously adaptive and very widely dispersed. But other species are already disappearing.

The Bramble Cay melomys was the first mammal species made extinct by climate change. A native Australian rodent, it lived only on a small, sandy cay in the northernmost part of the Great Barrier Reef – like the one I visited in 2018. Scientists had visited Bramble

Cay in 2014 to have a comprehensive look, but not a single melomys was seen, nor any tracks, nor any scats. Not only was the rat gone, but the amount of vegetation on the cay was down from multiple hectares to fractions of a hectare. The scientists blame sea level rises: 'The key factor responsible for the extirpation of this population was almost certainly ocean inundation of the low-lying cay, very likely on multiple occasions, during the last decade, causing dramatic habitat loss and perhaps also direct mortality of individuals.'[6]

To put it bluntly, the loss of a single vulnerable rodent species is unlikely to cause much wailing and lamentation. Neither will it tip the global ecosystem into precipitous spiralling collapse. But the melomys's role in this tale is a signal of everything that is at risk.

Now, it is quite possible some areas on earth will become more fecund because of climate change. Some temperate areas might become rainforest, for example. Some species might thrive. Some cities might improve. (London in particular could be absolutely lovely if it were five degrees warmer all year round.)

But the game of chance we'd be playing if we continued to invite these outcomes is a horrible one. We could leave whole nations stranded in dry arid belts, while the newly habitable parts of the world might be far away. Some parts of Australia are already hard to live in at some times of year, but our now-regular heatwaves are not even the most noticeable effect of climate change. That honour goes to the increase in extreme weather events. Some scientists believe extra energy in the atmosphere will increase the frequency of events that expend this energy. Endless storms, hurricanes or cyclones could really screw things up, even before the globe turns into a sauna.

New York City got blasted by Hurricane Sandy in 2012, and it also appears to be experiencing heavier than normal snow in recent winters. Records going back more than 150 years show that six of the biggest 10 snowstorms in NYC history are from the last 20 years.

The biggest – 27.5 inches (70 centimetres) of snow, as measured in Central Park – fell in January 2016.[7] That sliver of land along the United States' Atlantic Coast is disproportionately influential. It contains a great part of the world's wealth and some of the world's most admired publishing and education industries, and is, of course, the seat of political power of the world's most powerful country. If residents of the north-eastern United States have regular firsthand experience of the effects of climate change, it could be a major impetus to actually, you know, doing something about it.

Antarctica

We touched on the Arctic Circle before, but the Arctic is just an icy drop in the ocean compared to Antarctica.

As mentioned, the big risk to rising sea levels is not sea ice but *land* ice – land ice doesn't regularly melt and reform, meaning that it if it does melt, we end up in scuba gear. And Antarctica has a lot of land ice.

It is easy to forgive people for not understanding just how big Antarctica is. Maps give us little indication of it. In fact, map-makers have a lot to answer for. About the only time I've ever seen this issue discussed was in an episode of *The West Wing*. In 1999, during its first season, *The West Wing* devoted an episode to wacky lobbyists who come to the White House. One group of lobbyists, the 'Cartographers for Social Equality', demand aggressive legislation against the Mercator Projection – the method of portraying our *spherical* globe on a two-dimensional map.

The Mercator Projection has advantages for navigation but it also distorts some parts of the map, making areas near the poles look far bigger than they are. Finland and Sweden do very well out of the Mercator Projection, while Indonesia and Nigeria are squeezed in.

The privilege of distension is not extended to Antarctica. Next time you encounter a printed map, look closely at the lines of latitude. Most likely the equator is closer to the bottom of the map than the top – in their lavish treatment of the northern hemisphere, the map-makers seem to have forgotten that there's still half a world to draw. What's more, they generally trim the last few degrees of latitude off the southern hemisphere. Antarctica is all but omitted, when in fact it is giant: twice the size of Australia, much bigger than the USA, nearly as big as South America. And – cue ominous music – it is covered in ice multiple kilometres thick.

Antarctica is considered a desert. Little precipitation falls there, but the snow that does flutter down turns to ice. It then pretty much goes nowhere. Glacial flow is slow enough that snow falling as ice in central Antarctica will take one hundred thousand years to reach the sea. The slow build-up means the ice can be up to 4 kilometres (2.5 miles) deep in some places. Most of the world's fresh water is locked up as ice crystals atop the Antarctic land mass.[8]

If all the ice on Antarctica and the rest of the world melted, sea levels would rise by an estimated 70 metres (230 feet).[9] That would obliterate all of Florida and most of northern Europe, and make Brazil's Amazon basin into a huge sea.

Luckily full catastrophic melting is an extreme event that remains all but impossible in the foreseeable future. However, the collapse of certain ice shelves near Antarctica's western edge is more plausible in the medium term and could see the sea level rise by several metres.

While recent science suggests Antarctica is losing over 200 billion tonnes of land ice every year,[10] the details are complicated. The smaller western section of the continent (the part south of the Americas) is losing over 150 billion tonnes of ice each year. The Antarctic Peninsula – the part that curls up towards Patagonia – is losing roughly 30 billion tonnes per year. That's the bad news. The good news is that the large eastern part of Antarctica (south of Australia) is probably not losing as much ice. It might even have gained ice in some recent years – the same study estimates it added 5 billion tonnes a year between 1992 and 2017. Some climate models suggest this is due to a compensating effect: as the world warms and there is more moisture in the air, snowfall might increase over Antarctica. But whether this will continue – or is even happening – is very unclear. In fact, another study suggests that east Antarctica is actually *losing* around 50 billion tons of ice a year.[11]

This is the nature of climate science. It comes with a lot of uncertainties.

The incentives we need

The uncertainties of climate change combined with the scale of the problem tend to induce inertia in many people. Out of the exceptions and doubts it is possible to craft a plausible-seeming narrative that excuses inaction. But inaction is a big risk. We should probably do *something*.

But what? To answer that question, we need to answer the question of why global warming has become a problem in the first place. What incentives are at work here? Why do we let carbon into the atmosphere? Why do we keep filling the atmosphere with matter that traps heat energy inside our atmosphere and turns polar bears to skin and bone?

Because we have an accidental incentive to do so. The low prices of the fuels that produce carbon as a side effect make them an easy choice for billions of people worldwide. Those fuels in turn run our power stations, our cars, and our modern lives in almost every respect.

Don't get the impression I am opposed to the provision of cheap energy. Far from it. I think those low prices are good as far as their primary effect goes. And the ingenuity that has made energy so cheap would have to impress anyone.

As a demonstration of the power of the price incentive to encourage human ingenuity, the coal and oil industries are unmatched. The steam engine, for example, was invented for the coal industry. And railroads too – vehicles running on tracks had never been deployed on any proper scale until the North of England began digging up vast quantities of coal and needed a way to get it all south. Oil extraction has been a similar source of invention. It has brought us not only massive disastrous oil spills but also big advances in pipeline technology. Every time we thought the resources were running low these companies came up with another way to find and extract them – fracking, anyone? These advances are awesome in the original sense of the term – inspiring fear as well as admiration.

These industries are very good at keeping energy prices affordable. But as we face an incentive to use these cheap fuels for their many benefits, we are also incentivised to release carbon. Another way to look at it is that we have a *missing* incentive not to do so. There is no powerful incentive to encourage us *not* to release carbon. The same types of missing incentive explain why the oceans are now full of plastic: plastic is cheap and there's little immediate cost to discarding it in places where it can get in the ocean.

None of these huge environmental problems have come about because individual humans are absurdly destructive or greedy. Each of us makes only a tiny contribution to these problems. And so even a tiny incentive applied to each of us could be sufficient to contain the problem. A surcharge of a few cents on the most carbon-intensive choices and an equally tiny discount on the least carbon-intensive choices could make a huge difference. But – in Australia at least – there isn't any such incentive.

Climate change is not a plot or a result of evil forces. I believe it is an accident of incentives, and something we can change, so long as we understand that. People – even ones who want to do the right thing – will mostly be guided by incentives. We buy what's cheap and easy and convenient. Governments and businesses need to make the carbon-friendly choices the cheapest, easiest and best.

There is a market in apps that will tell you what to eat, wear and drive in order to minimise your carbon footprint. 'Be a Climate Hero!' says the advertising copy for Oroeco, which ranks your carbon footprint against others and encourages you to buy carbon credits. But Oroeco has only been installed by a few thousand users. Most people are too busy living their lives to also be a Climate Hero.

Putting the burden on people to police the carbon intensity of their lifestyle choices risks being both ineffective and unfair. Just like healthy eating, people who have a lot of capacity to make good choices can end up pointing their fingers at people with less capacity and blaming them. Tesla drivers may feel utterly superior to someone driving a 20-year-old car with the kind of fuel efficiency that came standard 20 years ago. But not everyone has the financial capacity to buy an electric car for A\$60,000. Similarly, people who own their home and install solar panels on the roof may scowl at the renters next door using the cheap power that comes down the wires.

The clean and green choices available to the typical Tesla driver and solar-panel owner are far greater than those available to other people. They can engage in a special kind of conspicuous consumption – one that is green tinged. Of course, a future where only the rich can make good choices (and not all the rich will) is not going to be effective. What's more, there's only so much due diligence a consumer can do. We must do far better than hoping everyone emulates the petit bourgeoisie by opting in to another version of luxury consumerism. Relying on mindful consumerism to solve climate change is like trying to cut down a tree by nibbling at the most delicate leaves. We need to take an axe to the trunk or, better yet, change the incentives at the root. Then we don't have to rely on anyone 'doing the right thing'. We can make people – even climate change deniers – reduce carbon emissions without even trying. The simplest and best way to do this is to turn the immense power of the price incentive back on us. To institute a carbon price.

A good carbon price will raise the price of emitting carbon until we limit emissions at levels that won't cause rising temperatures. This incentive should work in both the ways a price incentive works – by making us buy low-carbon products, and by making suppliers innovate until their products are low-carbon.

There are two carbon price methods. You can either make one directly with a carbon tax, or let the market come up with one by setting a limit on carbon emissions and creating a demand for emission permits, a process known as 'cap and trade'. The overall effect on carbon emissions should be similar, while the difference is in what is locked down – a tax provides certainty on price; cap and trade provides certainty on volume of carbon emitted.

Cap and trade is the theoretical winner. It gets the work of emissions reduction done by the parties that can most easily afford to reduce their emissions. For example, imagine you are a doughnut entrepreneur in a country where the government has just set up a cap and trade scheme. Imagine the government has given you some carbon permits for the power you use in frying those delicious treats. You face a choice. Do you carry on as you are, or try to reduce your carbon emissions and sell the permits for money?

If your doughnut company could easily swap to using solar power, you can sell off your permits and go solar. You don't need the permits anymore because your energy is clean and green. Those permits get bought by a doughnut-hole company that for some reason finds it hard to go solar. This is the magic of a cap and trade system. It causes a market in carbon credits to be created. The carbon reductions built into the permits are achieved without substantially reducing output of doughnuts or their holes.

On paper, it's a good scheme. But it creates a lot of opportunities for sneaky behaviour.

The first problem with cap and trade schemes is giving out the permits. If you announce that you will give permits to the polluters (as in our example above) you have a tricky incentive. All the doughnut shops will have an incentive to increase pollution in the period where you are measuring pollution output. Companies will do whatever they can to get their hands on more permits, even if that means creating more pollution. A classic perverse incentive.

Auctioning the permits is a better idea. Companies that know they can cut their carbon emissions cheaply will do that instead of bidding high at auction. But an auction is expensive for industries that would need to buy a lot of permits. Can governments resist subsidising permits when sectors cry poor? If electricity companies hint that there might be more blackouts, the government may be tempted to hand out permits for free. There is a substantial risk of corporate welfare here.

On the other hand, a carbon tax is less theoretically beautiful than cap and trade. It provides a blunt fixed-price incentive for everyone to cut their carbon output. The upside is that revenue flows to the government, meaning that revenue can be distributed around society to help smooth the introduction of the tax. But of course it suffers from branding issues – nobody likes to pay a new tax.

Carbon tax opponents say that it will kill our energy-intensive economies. Is that true? Early evidence says no. Carbon taxes have been introduced in a number of countries and states. So have emissions trading schemes. Sweden's carbon tax is a staggering €114 per tonne.[12] But it works. Volvo has recently opened a carbon neutral manufacturing plant in the country. Swedish carbon emissions are 26 per cent below their 1990 levels[13] and, with one of the highest GDPs per capita in Europe, its economy is fitter than a bull elk.

The trading game

The history of carbon policy is really quite quick. We've come from nothing in a few decades. The story arguably starts at the G7 meeting in 1989, where the seven powerful economies represented called for action on the 'excessive emissions of carbon dioxide and other greenhouse gases which could lead to future climate changes'.[14]

Next, in 1992, a UN conference in Rio de Janeiro created the UN Framework Convention on Climate Change. This convention – still in existence – has been surprisingly powerful, not because it put some insipid non-binding carbon emission limits on countries, but because it involved a lot of follow-up meetings. And at one of those meetings in 1997, deep in the northern suburbs of the Japanese city of Kyoto, the Kyoto Protocol was decided. *This* protocol was widely agreed to be the first major step taken towards combatting climate change.

The Kyoto Protocol got countries to agree to get emissions down to 5 per cent below 1990 levels by 2008.[15] Countries were free to figure out how. One option was to pay for credits produced elsewhere, which is where we get our first example of how cap and trade can go pear-shaped.

Under the Kyoto Protocol, a large and peculiar emissions trading scheme was set up. The Clean Development Mechanism allowed rich countries to buy carbon emission permits ('carbon offsets') by sponsoring projects in developing countries. It created some great projects, like tree planting in India. But eventually it was abandoned in despair.

The problem with carbon offsets starts at the most conceptual level. An offset requires paying people to do or not do things. But those things might have happened anyway.

Say I want to pay people to *not* cut down trees. Say you own lots of trees and you had no plan to cut them down. It may be possible for you to pretend you fully intended to cut them down in order to claim a payment. Of course bureaucrats in charge of schemes demand proof. But proof is easy to manufacture if you have a few consultants on tap to do some 'modelling' and show off their Microsoft PowerPoint skills.

When you create an incentive for people to act in a way they would not have acted otherwise, you have created an incentive for a pile of lies that will reach the skies. You never know what would have happened otherwise (accurate counter-factual scenarios remain one of the world's most elusive substances).

Unsurprisingly, the market for carbon offsets under the Clean Development Mechanism was soon crawling with corruption.

One of the most outrageous carbon abatement scandals was set in the Russian city of Kirov. Kirov? It's sort of near Kazan. That mean much to you? No? Near Ufa …? Let's just say Kirov is near large expanses of Siberian forest.

In Kirov there is an old Soviet factory for making refrigerants, now owned by a company called HaloPolymer. In 2012 their halo slipped and the company started doing something rather sneaky.

The making of refrigerants produces a lot of greenhouse gases. One by-product in particular is a real stone in our shoe: HFC-23. This hydrofluorocarbon is small but mighty. HFC-23, weight for weight, is 11,700 times more powerful a greenhouse gas than carbon dioxide. Trapping just one tonne of it is extremely valuable for reducing total greenhouse gas emissions. The Kirov plant produced plenty of HFC-23. But with the introduction of a pretty simple incinerator, the offending molecule could be neutralised. HaloPolymer signed up to get credits for eliminating it.

The trouble was that the amount of HFC-23 being incinerated suddenly went up. According to a 2015 letter to the journal *Nature Climate Change*, the plant's operators 'increased waste gas generation to unprecedented levels once they could generate credits from producing more waste gas.'[16] Scientists published graphs of HFC-23 production at the plant and were able to show that it peaked outrageously when they were able to claim extra credits for it. Importantly, those peaks were not caused by increased output of actual refrigerants.

The Kirov plant was not the only plant in Russia to follow such an approach. The incentives to game the system were strong – worth millions of euros in revenue – and the technical challenge was insignificant.

The Clean Development Mechanism is not alone as a troubled carbon-trading system. The EU's own carbon-trading system – while at least still in existence today – has had its share of scandals. One measure of its failure is the current price of carbon – well under €1 per tonne. Sadly now few people take the system terribly seriously.

The market for voluntary carbon offsets is even murkier. Voluntary carbon offsets are credits that can be purchased outside regulated trading mechanisms in order to claim that an activity is carbon neutral. One famous example is a project called the Vatican Forest. In 2007 the Vatican was gifted a lot of credits by a carbon permit vendor in order to allow the Vatican to become carbon neutral. Land in Hungary was set aside for a forest to back those credits. But no trees were ever planted.[17] The vacant land is a metaphor for the promise of carbon trading overall: it seems so promising, but it is very hard to get the incentives to grow in the way you want.

Australia's short-lived carbon tax was intended to eventually transform to an emissions trading scheme. Australia had a carbon tax for 730 days, between 1 July 2012 and 1 July 2014. Carbon emissions from electricity generation fell by around 9 per cent in six months.[18] Overall, even though Australia's economy and population grew, carbon emissions were roughly stable at around 130 megatons every three months. In 2013 a new government was elected and the tax was repealed, beginning in 2014. Thereafter carbon emissions grew again to around 134 megatons every three months.[19] The tax ended before the transition to cap and trade could happen, but that may have avoided some disasters.

This book obviously champions deploying incentives to get things done. But it is also about the complexity and risk of incentive schemes. Incentives rarely work exactly as you think they will. You have to keep changing the rules to get the outcomes you desire. Like anyone who runs an incentive scheme, people who run carbon markets need to be hyper vigilant.

Risk

We may have to admit a partial and temporary defeat on global carbon trading. The perverse incentives created under widespread carbon trading may for now be too complex to control. It appears to be working in certain circumstances – such as within well-regulated high-trust societies in northern Europe, and if limited to projects of a certain size and scope. Beyond that, the risks amplify dramatically.

But we should keep trying carbon trading. It has vast potential; we just need to tread very carefully. Politicians in the field thinking of something other than incentives – deliberate or accidental – will fail.

A carbon tax is less theoretically elegant and less economically efficient than cap and trade. But it is far simpler and has far fewer facets that interested parties can chip away at in search of advantage. A carbon tax may a good way to move forward without massive scandal, waste and eventual environmental disaster.

While carbon trading is exceedingly complex, carbon taxing is not without difficulties. Essentially, putting a cost on carbon is not costless. Those impacted – including powerful companies – can band together and fight against it. Any politician who journeys to set up a carbon tax needs to be intrepid. There is treasure in the temple of incentives, but the path to it is strewn with the skeletons of those who tried before you.

And it's not just powerful profit-making entities that resist such changes. Carbon taxes have the potential to impact everyday people, and everyday people do not like seeing their incentives change either. In Australia, the fight over a carbon tax has coincided with the premature incineration of the political careers of about half-a-dozen prime ministers. In the US the issue is also a political tinderbox. During the writing of this book, a protest movement in France – the *Gilets Jaunes* – started burning things down like it was 1789 all over again, this time in fury over a carbon tax.

The smoke over the Champs-Élysées should remind us that changing incentives is serious. Incentives are part of our cultures and systems. Changing incentives means changing our cultures and systems. Think of all those French autoroutes and all the Peugeots on them – they were built under a different incentive scheme, one that encourages driving. If French prime minister Emmanuel Macron changes the incentives around buying fuel, he makes those roads and Peugeots harder and more expensive to use. Of course there is anger.

But we can also find reasons to hope. Incentive design can not only make a policy cause for rebellion; it can also help with acceptance. Sometimes a spoonful of sugar helps the medicine go down. An international lobby group called the Climate Leadership Council has an idea for that sugar – carbon dividends that pay out directly to citizens. In Australia these dividends could be A$1300 per adult per year according to one estimate.[20] And you'd receive them by virtue of being a citizen. I like the idea. Australia used a similar sweetener to grease the wheels of the failed carbon tax, but it was disguised and dispersed across taxing and spending programs. That's hard to notice. A fat dividend in your bank account, by contrast, is powerful.

What if it works?

Why is doing something about climate change the low-risk option? Not because global markets are weak, but because they are strong.

Claims that a carbon tax will ruin the global economy seem to me absurd. Have the people making those claims ever seen a market economy? It's the most powerful machine ever invented for figuring out solutions and bringing them to life.

Once the right incentives are in place, human ingenuity gets to work. We are likely to discover we can quite easily conserve energy in some places – for example, we've already seen fuel economy gradually improve from 10 litres per 100 kilometres to under 8 litres, and then take a big leap with hybrid vehicles, some of which use less than 4 litres of fuel per 100 kilometres. In other places we will be able to create energy without emitting carbon – solar power is just one option here. With the right incentives in place, these choices will start to seem obvious. And as the UN fights over climate policy, the price of renewable power and storage may fall so steeply that it becomes an economically better choice, below the price of new coal plants – and it is already very close in many places. Even absent policy, this would help us make big steps toward avoiding climate change.

If incentives help create a solution that allows us to cut carbon emissions cheaply then a lot of other traditional economic activity may continue seemingly unaffected. Such a solution might actually disappoint some people if, for example, they thought by supporting a carbon tax they would effect widespread change and create an environment free of consumerism.

Ending consumerism, while a worthy pursuit, is an awful lot to ask. I rather suspect a carbon-neutral world will still involve a lot of SUVs rolling through the McDonalds drive-through in an urban sprawl of enormous houses. The differences will be almost invisible: the SUVs run on a battery. The Big Macs are made with artificial meat. The enormous houses have insulation and solar panels. And none of those are mindful choices – they're just the obvious choices. The ones the incentives push everyone towards.

Demanding the world change its whole lifestyle is a much harder ask than simply shifting the incentives slightly so that most of the same activities can go on with much less of the damaging side effects. I think we will still buy things in shops that look much the same, live in houses that feel much the same and drive cars that are operated in much the same way. Would such a future be a horror scenario or a triumph? I call it a triumph. It would not show that carbon pricing has failed but that it has worked so well as to remain almost invisible. It would show that deploying a price incentive works like a scalpel. It would demonstrate that a carbon price can help solve the carbon intensity of the global economy without disrupting everything else. That's a hopeful vision for anyone who wants the Great Barrier Reef to be there for the next generation and the one thereafter.

As I write this, Australia is experiencing a heatwave with temperatures in vast areas close to 50 degrees Centigrade (122 degrees Fahrenheit). Days like that create blackouts, and sure enough all the houses in my area of Melbourne lost power. On the hottest day of the year, with the fans motionless and the air-conditioning silent,

I collapsed on the floorboards in our windowless hallway to get away from the heat. The dog lay next to me, panting. As I sheltered from the heat and parts of the country hit new record temperatures, the risks of inaction on climate change seemed awfully high.

In the long run, I am optimistic about the power of incentives and the power of markets. People who believe in markets should be the champions of climate action – the power of price incentives is to help us solve problems exactly like this, and solve them efficiently. If we let a price incentive loose, alternatives to carbon-emitting activities that don't suffer from diminishing returns to scale are likely to eventually become pretty cheap, and a global price on carbon could end up being surprisingly low. After all, a good incentive doesn't have to be huge to create an enormous aggregate effect.

Chapter 14

Ostrom

Every book needs a hero to come in at the end and save the day. Ours is not Katniss Everdeen. Ours is a polite Californian woman named Elinor Ostrom, and she will teach us something profound about incentives.

Elinor Ostrom was born in 1933 in Los Angeles amid the depths of the Great Depression. Her father left not long later. The household was poor. Elinor Ostrom's mother, a musician, put a high value on the household growing their own vegetables, and a low value on college education. But Ostrom was a very capable student. By a quirk of geography, she attended a high school full of wealthy students – Beverly Hills High School. She did well in school, and upon finishing, could see no reason not to do what all her classmates were doing, so she applied for college, even though her mother would not support her in doing so.

Ostrom was admitted at the University of California, Los Angeles, in 1951. As a student, Ostrom took many jobs to support herself. I'm sure no one who walked into the Los Angeles dime store would've guessed the 19-year-old behind the counter would be a future winner of a Nobel Prize for economics. (This is not one of the original prizes set up by Alfred Nobel and funded from his fortune, but don't listen to the physicists – being funded by the Bank of Sweden does not make the economics prize any less legitimate!)

Ostrom excelled in college and graduated into an American economy that had recovered from the Great Depression then boomed after World War II. But the Los Angeles job market in the 1950s did not have tremendous opportunities for everyone. Ostrom found it 'somewhat of a shock to me to have future employers immediately ask whether I had typing and shorthand skills. The presumption in those days was that the appropriate job for a woman was as a secretary or as a teacher'.[1]

Ostrom was eventually hired by a large exports firm to do … typing and shorthand. But she knew well these were not the limit of her capabilities. After a few years of work she dipped her toes back into the academic world, then eventually applied for a PhD in economics.

The UCLA Economics Department said no, because the education system that had discouraged a young female student from taking the advanced mathematics now required it as a condition of progress.

Nevertheless, Ostrom persisted. She enrolled in a political science PhD instead. Even there, the odds were not in favour of a young woman. Of her class of 40 PhD students, 37 were men. 'We were told after we began our program that the faculty had a very heated meeting in which they criticized the Departmental Committee for admitting any women,' Ostrom said.[2]

It was apparently thought that a PhD graduate's eventual career reflected on the school, and because women would obviously have less impressive careers, admitting them to the program would make UCLA look bad. Quite the self-perpetuating incentive system.

The UCLA political science department was at the time fervently studying the way California's water use was being governed. Elinor Ostrom was roped into this research effort, and so began a voyage of discovery that would eventually see her accepting a golden medallion from the hand of the King of Sweden.

Ostrom's award-winning research was on situations that could develop into 'tragedies of the commons': where some fragile common resource gets overused until that resource is destroyed for everyone. For example, Californian water.

Southern California sees little rainfall each year. The Pacific Ocean is not much use for drinking. So the greatest supply of water is groundwater. Water sits underground in the rocks below Los Angeles is gigantic quantities. Nobody owns it. Anyone can get it by pumping or by digging wells. It's the perfect setting for a tragedy of the commons. People could pump that reservoir out till it was dry, and there was no incentive on any of them to stop.

But Elinor Ostrom did not find her way into this book by simply confirming the well-established economic dictum that we humans are prone to get trapped in such dilemmas. Quite the reverse. She worked for decades to find the incentive systems to manage these situations. And Ostrom was not bound by pre-existing paradigms. She did her own thinking.

Triumph of the commons

Ostrom lived through a terribly exciting period in Californian history, hydrologically speaking. California was growing fast and by the 1940s its water resources were being mercilessly exploited and degraded. Millions of litres were being taken out of the underground aquifers each month. As the fresh water levels fell, the Pacific Ocean had begun to flow in. Seawater incursion threatened to permanently destroy the precious reserves.

But as Ostrom observed, this situation changed. Water users banded together. They formed committees. They self-organised.

They surveyed the situation. They forged agreements. They created rules and systems. They put those rules and systems in place. They all started taking much less water from underground aquifers.

The water level stopped dropping and began to rise back to its natural level. A complete reversal.

Economics has two very simple models it loves to use for explaining human behaviour. One is the tragedy of the commons. The second is the prisoner's dilemma. The prisoner's dilemma asks you to imagine two prisoners who committed a serious crime together and are now being interrogated separately. Each knows the other is under pressure to confess. And if one criminal confesses, then the other not confessing is a bad option – they get punished while their conspirator gets leniency. Both prisoners not only know the incentives – they know that the other knows that they face the *same* incentives. Most versions of the prisoner's dilemma show that both prisoners end up confessing.

Both of these models are examples of game theory – the study of how people interact in strategic situations. And both are quite pessimistic about people's capacity to coordinate.

Ostrom realised that neither model described the situation in California. The tragedy of the commons says such situations end in a destroyed resource, but the Californian aquifers were saved. Ostrom saw that economics had a blind spot.

Part of the problem was an over-reliance on simple models. Ostrom was very suspicious of any model that fitted every situation with little effort expounded: 'The intellectual trap in relying entirely on models to provide the foundation for policy analysis is that scholars then presume that they are omniscient observers able to comprehend the essentials of how complex dynamic systems work by creating stylised descriptions of some aspects of those systems.'[3]

Of course, the belief that a person has omniscience – the power of being all-seeing – is the biggest risk in any intellectual pursuit. Because once you think you see it all clearly, you stop really looking. If you are sure that a commons is prone to tragedy, you can fail to see what is happening before your very eyes.

Ostrom has a particular dislike for the prisoner's dilemma. 'As long as individuals are viewed as prisoners, policy prescriptions will address this metaphor,' she writes.[4]

This is Ostrom's insight: we are not only capable of being victims of incentives, but we are capable of being the authors too. And this doesn't just mean seizing a blank slate through revolution. Ostrom instead describes how people write incentives within an existing system.

We know that governments can make new incentives. We know entrepreneurs and business owners can create incentives. But Ostrom described groups forging and maintaining systems of incentives – often ones that had no legal force – and agreeing to abide by them.

There are many places her ideas are relevant. You might find yourself part of a neighbourhood group on Facebook that sets up rules to manage local parking better. Or you might belong to a resident's association that creates rules to manage the upkeep of a communal garden. Perhaps you're involved in an online community that manages to create incentives that create and maintain an enormous common resource (like Wikipedia, for example).

All these are easy-to-see examples of Ostrom's principles in practice. But we can also apply them at the global level. After all, at a global level there is neither a single corporate structure nor a single government and many very pressing incentive problems to solve.

The systems Ostrom studied contain some absolutely inspired incentives. My favourite comes from the poor farmers of the

Philippines. Their big problem is water. They need it to grow crops and they rely on irrigation canals to bring water to their land.

Irrigation requires great self-control. Canals are a one-way street: water comes in at the top and gets taken out as it flows down. Upstream farmers must stand by and watch perfectly good water flow right past their property, because that water will be claimed by farmers downstream. There is a tremendous and ever-present risk that the farmers upstream will take more water than they are allocated, leaving none for the farmers downstream.

The solution is brilliant – the Filipino farmers divide up the land so everybody farms some land upstream, some land midstream and some land downstream. The block of land right at the very end goes to the most senior farmer – the one whose job it is to manage the canal. If everyone upstream is pumping more water than they should, the farmer will find out. In this way the farmers created a system that provides its own incentives and they all get enough water to grow the crops they need to survive. It's beautiful in its simplicity.

This system is not put in place by a company. It is not put in place by a government. It is created by a collective of people. An irrigation canal is a classic example of a common resource that could become a tragedy of the commons – if everyone takes too much water then there is none left for anybody. The people who depend on the resource recognise the problem and come up with ways to solve it themselves.

What Ostrom couldn't help but notice is that mainstream economics had not tried to explain this phenomenon.

Why can economics not see that people can change the rules? Perhaps it has to do with how economic models work. Existing models show economists how people will respond under certain circumstances, for example, how people will react if a price goes up. But the people *in* the model never get to fiddle with the model. That's the economist's job. The economist can be lulled into assuming that in the real world only external impetus can change a situation.

Economic models like to distinguish things that change – 'endo-genous factors' – and things that are fixed – 'exogenous factors'. This is indispensable for simplifying analysis. But in the real world, nothing is permanently fixed and everything is endogenous – even the rules governing a situation.

The game includes the meta game

Imagine if one of the rules of Scrabble was that you get to change the rules of Scrabble once per game, if everyone agrees. That is the kind of situation the real world offers. Sometimes it is possible for people facing incentives to band together and tweak them, or even completely upend them. They can do this through established demo-cratic processes – or revolution. But as Ostrom shows, that is often not necessary, and many triumphs of the commons were achieved in times and places where formal democracy was not a factor

Ostrom observed that the groups that rallied around three major Californian water basins used three similar but different approaches to successfully get their water exploitation situation under control. Three times, she saw the tragedy of the commons turn into triumph, so she went looking for other such examples. She saw it in the Philippines with the irrigation canals, and she kept seeing it.

She found Swiss villages where elaborate rules kept the alpine meadows from being exploited. And Japanese villages that kept people from pillaging the local forests through a system of rules complete with detectives on horseback and fines that had to be paid in *sake*.

This was not normal economic research. Perhaps not studying all that mathematics freed Ostrom from the constraints of the discipline.

She realised that most cited studies in economics came from within the economic discipline, if not from the same sector or region, and so therefore ignored practical applications. She instead spent years delving into diverse case studies from all over the world, looking at 'rural sociology, anthropology, history, economics, political science, forestry, irrigation sociology, and human ecology'.[5] And in this grab bag, Ostrom realised she had uncovered a gold mine.

In her seminal 1990 book, *Governing the Commons*, Elinor Ostrom is particularly cruel to the fundamentalists. She loves to quote academic theorists who insist on definitive answers like 'the only solution to problem X is the allocation of private property rights' and immediately prove them wrong with a description of a group of people banding together to solve problem X without formal property rights. The only thing she might actually enjoy more than that it is to quote theorists who insist 'the only solution to problem Y is government intervention' and debunk them.

Ostrom's great strength is her love of shades of grey. Her favourite clause is 'it depends', and her enemies are the fundamentalist ideologies that plague both ends of the economic spectrum. Fundamentalism pretends to great insight but it is, in truth, intellectual weakness. The desire to apply one rule in a range of circumstances is an admission of an inability to grasp the variation in circumstances, and an unwillingness to try. The usefulness of any idea or theory depends on features of the world that will be present in some situations but not others. When people lack the curiosity or capacity to sniff out those features, they revert to fundamentalism.

Understanding incentives is not about fundamentalism. On the contrary, it is about doubt, contingent thinking, 'if/then'-ing, muddling through and tinkering. It's about making up your mind only when a decision is absolutely necessary, then immediately being open to information on whether the decision was right or wrong.

Incentives require a love for details and they don't permit much fundamentalism because to keep in control of them you need to be constantly open to seeing new ways they can be exploited.

Huertas and zanjeras

Botany and gravity are enemies. Plants need water to grow, and gravity means water only flows downhill. If it wasn't for those annoying conditions, irrigation wouldn't even be necessary. It is, however, vital to life in dry regions of the world, and so farmers must invest time and money in the maintenance of irrigation systems.

Let's go back to the Philippines, 500 kilometres north of Manila, where a federation of nine irrigation systems – *zanjeras* – depends on a dam that gets washed away at least once every year, sometimes more.

Elinor Ostrom describes the process of rebuilding it like this:

> *Rebuilding takes about a week – somewhat more when the weather is unfavourable – and involves several hundred persons. Each zanjera is responsible for bringing construction materials and providing work teams (and the cooks and food to feed them). After spending a day preparing banana and bamboo mats, work teams in heavy boats confront the swirling waters to begin pounding in the poles that form the foundation for the dam.*[6]

There is a clear danger here – and I'm not talking about the swirling waters. The best strategy, in a game theory sense is to let the other farmers in the other zanjeras build the dam while you stay home and cultivate your field. These people are desperately poor and they can't easily afford to give up the yield of an extra week tilling the fields. But instead, attendance at the dam rebuilding is 94 per cent. Why?

Simple – fines are levied for non-attendance. This punishment works so well because offenders don't need to be chased down. This is not a complex punishment to administer at all. Everyone can observe whether you show up to help build the dam or not.

Building the dams requires large amounts of unpaid work. And that's without mentioning the maintenance that has to happen on the canals. In total, membership in a zanjera requires contributing an average of 39 days of work a year per person to the common good. Which makes your local school 'working bee' look like a picnic.

The burdens on farmers are high and the incentive structures that demand so much of them may appear fragile. But the zanjeras have survived a long time. Modern water experts have assessed them and found they do not meet the highest standards for water-use efficiency, but the engineering question is not the one they are optimised to solve. The important thing about irrigation systems, it turns out, is not the engineering behind the sluice gates or the mathematics of evaporation rates. The hydrology is a doddle compared to the incentives.

Outside the apostles door, each Thursday

The Tribunal de las Aguas de la Vega de Valencia (Water Tribunal of the Plain of Valencia) has been around so long, nobody is actually sure when it started. The best theory is it dates back over 1000 years to the Moorish period of Spain – which would explain why the court has many features of Islamic law.

The tribunal is a group of eight farmers, elected by other farmers in the region, who meet every Thursday outside the Apostles door of the cathedral of Valencia. They can meet outside because it so rarely rains in Valencia. That is also why the tribunal is so important. Each farmer comes from a separate irrigation channel where they, with a few dedicated staff, are in charge of enforcing the rules. At the tribunal they represent the thousand-plus farmers who live along their channel.

The eight farmers don black robes, pull up a circle of chairs and, as the bell in church tower above strikes noon, begin to thrash out the problems of the irrigators from the hot dry plain of Valencia. And they do it without lawyers. The tribunal is not official but it tries cases and issues fines. It also acts as a tiny representative body – setting down rules and at times sending petitions to Madrid.

The tribunal is the crucial moving part of an incentive system that has defused a potential disaster – a tragedy of the commons situation that could starve half of eastern Spain if water were misallocated. The tribunal has outlasted Moorish, Regal and Fascist control of Spain, survived the Black Plague, the Spanish Flu and the Civil War, and has remained in place despite the industrial revolution and the advent of the European Union.

If you go to Valencia you can go and listen, but a warning: proceedings happen in Valencian dialect. Even if you speak Spanish, it may be hard to follow what happens. It keeps no written records. Such a system might sound ripe for corruption, but its longevity suggests otherwise.

The existence of this court is not a side effect or an amusing quirk of the fact that the Spanish have successfully inhabited the region for so long. It is a reason that they have done so. Without an appropriate system of water management, agriculture would be difficult and conflict would arise. This incentive system – the rules and punishments it enforces – is working. It has worked for a long time.

The courts are not the only feature of these systems. They are designed minutely from the ground up with features that shape the incentives of participants in order to take only a fair amount of water, even if that hurts their crops and especially under circumstances when that is the case.

One key feature of the system is that the actions of farmers are relatively easy for other farmers to see. The farms are small – many less than a hectare. Usually the farmers stand on the edge of field waiting to open a gate and let water into their fields when their time comes. At that moment they can often see the next door farmer standing in his field, and if he doesn't close the gate to stop water at the exact right moment, it is immediately apparent.

This layer of monitoring is an accidental structure provided by the small farms, but it means that even though fines issued by the court for water theft are small, theft is unlikely to be profitable. There are strong incentives not to take more water than is permitted.

High levels of monitoring are vital for applying punishments. If there is a low chance of evading detection, fines don't need to be large. When the high levels of monitoring can be pro bono by other interested parties, you have a system that is cheap to run and has a good chance of being self-sustaining. Although making a system that lasts as long as the Tribunal de las Aguas is not guaranteed!

The tribunal is not the only such court in the region. In nearby Murcia, the *huerta* (agricultural area) depends on the Consejo de Hombres Buenos (Council of Wise Men), which works in similar fashion to the Tribunal de las Aguas. Alicante and Orihuela also have huertas that employ similar rules and structures.

These systems show us how successful incentives can be, when properly combined. Systems often work well when each layer watches another layer, making every person accountable to another. Transparency is paramount. It is a key feature of the huertas and the zanjeras, and it is why they have been able to turn tragedy to triumph for centuries.

Importantly, Ostrom also catalogues those systems that fail: a Californian water basin that failed to sort itself out. Sri Lankan irrigation systems that are barely functional. A Sri Lankan fishing community that collapsed. What many of these failed systems have in common is excessive centralisation. Instead of locating power at the low levels and building up from below, power is applied from above by governments that may upset delicate local balances or set rules that are not sensitive to local conditions.

If you're in a top-down incentive system that is not working, Ostrom's message is to not give up. Success is possible, she says. We can break the traps that face us, by paying very close attention to the design of the systems of incentives. She describes a good system as one that will 'bring out the best in humans'.[7]

That's what incentives are for. Humans are capable of inspirational displays of brilliance. Flashes of genius. Gritty, drawn-out demonstrations of self-control. But not always. Human brilliance can get blocked and inhibited. We can, as a group – *especially* as a group – behave less than perfectly. The best behaviour of humans often needs to be tempted out with the right kind of incentives.

Conclusion

That Ball is Still in the Air

Remember the ball my father threw into the air? That's quite a good metaphor for all the things that could come crashing down around us. All the problems we face at home, at work and in wider society. And the small, hapless boy entrusted with catching the ball? He stands for all the people trying their hardest to do the right thing, and frequently failing.

Despair is understandable when we look at the world as it is. But this book hopes to act as an antidote. We need not simply expect the metaphorical ball to spill onto the grass. We should not blame ill intent if it does. We can believe in a better outcome.

Every story – from the convicts heading to Australia to the coders at Kaggle – demonstrates that we can identify incentives that determine what happens, for good and for ill. Often enough, we can start to control them. And the more we grasp the details of incentives, the better our efforts will be.

As we know, incentives are all about thinking naive and acting cynical. The ability to be more naively idealistic is granted by understanding reward and punishment, and their power. Once we accept that power, there is room for a dramatically bigger conception of what sort of outcomes are possible.

Combining naivety and cynicism might sound odd. Why be idealistic if the world's path is determined by the shape of incentives? The whole point of identifying accidental incentives is to emphasise how much 'destiny' is formed by side effects of systems that are under our control. What *is* and what *has to be* are not the same.

Getting our naivety and our cynicism in the right order is vital. If we are cynical about the possibility of change and naive about how to make it happen, we've got everything backwards. We will oscillate between despair and doomed quixotic campaigns to alter behaviour.

Imagine I buy myself a healthy-eating cookbook but make no other changes to my life. The cookbook doesn't change my incentives at all, and it won't be long before I am slumped dejectedly on the couch devouring chips. But resignation to my fate is entirely unnecessary. I need to tap into more hope for what's possible (say, a magazine-quality sixpack) and far more cynicism about what will make that possibility a reality (for example, donating to a cause I don't believe in if the kilos aren't falling off).

The same is true whether you're trying to manage a team at work, investing in a cryptocurrency, or voting for plans to combat climate change. Every smart person can see better ways to get things done, but don't just hope everyone will suddenly 'see the light' and adopt those better ways. Don't despair if people don't spontaneously behave as you want them to. Do believe you can obtain that better outcome with the right incentives, and remember that what counts as the right incentives will probably change over time.

If you're responsible for designing an incentive system, be prepared to tweak and re-tweak, assess and re-assess. If you're subject to an incentive system, the same applies, but with greater – though not insurmountable – challenges.

Belief in the power of incentives doesn't mean taking a sunshine-and-moonbeams attitude about the process of getting them to work.

Quite the reverse. Fierce cynicism is needed to keep those incentives from being exploited and decaying into something unwanted. Whether you're training your dog or analysing forensic evidence, intense monitoring and fast reactions are needed to prevent problems.

This book doesn't just aim to give you insights into incentives, but to increase your ability and confidence to make your own insights. Understanding incentives gives you a superpower: a theoretical framework that can help you see the way the world works with more clarity. Incentives don't explain everything, and they aren't the only system at work in human behaviour, but this framework allows you to make better predictions about how people will act. It won't be long before you start to recognise incentives in action – accidental, perverse, failing, succeeding, unnoticed or hiding in plain sight – everywhere you look. You will notice a curious cluster of behaviour and be able to trace the thread back. Eventually you will find some odd system spitting incentives. And you might even be able to change it.

When you see a system working well, examine the incentives at play and learn from them. When you see a problem, try to do the same. Don't fall for the trap of assigning all the blame to the character of the person. After all, bad scientists operate in a system that publishes bad science. Crooked cops work in a system that gives promotions to crooked cops.

Whether you're acting as a citizen, an investor, a parent, dog-owner, manager, or just trying to change your own behaviour, having a tight grasp of incentives will make your actions far more effective. Your vote, your money, your time and effort will all be best deployed when you understand their power and limitations.

If you can imagine a better scenario, you can begin to engineer it with better incentives. Think naive – 'you can catch the ball' – and act cynical – 'I'll give you a dollar if you do'. The rewards could be enormous.

Acknowledgements

Writing a book for the first time is like putting together IKEA furniture – it is far harder and takes a lot longer than you expected. The amount of support needed to make it to the end is huge, and acknowledgment of all that support is very much due.

Thank you to the many smart people who helped with this book and shaped the ideas in it. Thanks to Eric Beecher for the impetus to write it. Special shout out to the members of my book club for convening to talk about something that hadn't even been written yet – you gave me hope that the idea made sense. Big thanks to my mother, father and sister for reading and providing feedback and support. Thanks to Arwen Summers and Emily Hart at Hardie Grant for their relentless positivity and terrific editing eyes. And most of all, thanks and love to Grace for huge patience, love and support throughout the whole process.

Endnotes

Introduction

1   Bentham, J, 1789, *An Introduction to the Principles of Morals and Legislation*
2   Dhyani, J, 2017, https://blog.jaibot.com/

Chapter 1: The Power of Incentives

1   Fryer, RG et al, 2017, 'Vertical versus horizontal incentives in education: evidence from randomized trials', The National Bureau of Economic Research
2   Munger, C, 1995, 'The psychology of human misjudgement'

Chapter 2: A Perverse Inclination

1   Vann, M, 2003, 'Of rats, rice, and race: the great Hanoi rat massacre, an episode in French colonial history', *French Colonial History*, vol. 4
2   Lorenz, T, 20 May 2018, 'Electric scooter charger culture is out of control', *The Atlantic*, https://www.theatlantic.com/technology/archive/2018/05/charging-electric-scooters-is-a-cutthroat-business/560747/?single_page=true
3   Chrystal, A and Mizen, P, 2003, 'Goodhart's Law: its origins, meanings and implications for monetary policy', *Central Banking, Monetary Theory and Practice*
4   Capparella, J, 3 January 2019, 'The best-selling cars, trucks and SUVs of 2018', *Car and Driver*, https://www.caranddriver.com/news/g25558401/best-selling-cars-suv-trucks-2018/

Chapter 3: Unintentional

1   Victorian Department of Education and Training, 2018, 'For parents: going to school', https://www.education.vic.gov.au/parents/going-to-school/Pages/zones-restrictions.aspx

2   Balwyn High School, 22 February 2019, *The Lion*
3   Australian Bureau of Statistics, 2016 Census, https://www.abs.gov.au/websitedbs/censushome.nsf/home/2016
4   Real Estate Institute of Victoria, 28 August 2017, 'Education hot spots driving house price growth', https://reiv.com.au/news-resources/latest-news/education-hot-spots-driving-house-price-growth
5   Walker, T, 24 February 2016, 'Balwyn High School in Melbourne sparks property boom as parents fight to get in', *Australian Financial Review*, https://www.afr.com/brand/afr-magazine/balwyn-high-school-in-melbourne-a-real-estate-boom-zone-20151116-gl027o

Chapter 4: Missing Incentives

1   Old Bailey Proceedings, 9 September 1789, 'Mary Desmond, Mary Butler. Theft: grand larceny', https://www.oldbaileyonline.org/browse.jsp?id=t17890909-14&div=t17890909-14
2   Keneally, T, 2005, *The Commonwealth of Thieves*
3   History Australia, 'Neptune 1790', http://www.historyaustralia.org.au/twconvic/Neptune+1790
4   Middleton, J, cited in Hyman, D, 2011, 'Convicts and convictions: some lessons from transportation for health reform', *University of Pennsylvania Law Review*
5   Wathen, J, Letter received from William Hill, Sydney Cove, Port Jackson, 26 July 1790 (copy made in 1791), State Library of NSW, http://digital.sl.nsw.gov.au/delivery/DeliveryManagerServlet?dps_pid=FL1066687&embedded=true&toolbar=false
6   Johnson, R, cited in Flannery, T (Ed.), 1999, *The Birth of Sydney*
7   Flynn, M, 2016, *The Dictionary of Sydney*
8   *The Times of London*, 18 November 1791, p. 3
9   Grose, F, 12 October 1793, 'Letter to Rt. Hon Henry Dundas', *Historical Record of Australia*, p. 454, https://nla.gov.au/nla.obj-472896848/view?partId=nla.obj-473248117#page/n485/mode/1up
10 Sturgess, G et al., 2016, 'Commissioning human services: lessons from Australian convict contracting', *Australian Journal of Public Administration*

Chapter 5: Your Brain on Incentives

1   Olds, J, cited in Thompson, R, 1999, *Biographical Memoirs*, vol. 77, National Academy of Sciences
2   Frank, RA and Stutz, RM, 1984, 'Self-deprivation: A review', *Psychological Bulletin*, vol. 6, no. 2
3   Loewi, O, 1960, 'An autobiographic sketch', *Perspectives in Biology and Medicine*, vol. 4, no. 1
4   Pecina, S et al., 2003, 'Hyperdopaminergic mutant mice have higher "wanting" but not "liking" for sweet rewards', *Journal of Neuroscience*, vol. 23, iss. 28, https://www.ncbi.nlm.nih.gov/pubmed/14561867/

5   Cousins, YMS and Salamone, JD, 1994, 'Nucleus accumbens dopamine depletions in rats affect relative response allocation in a novel cost/benefit procedure', *Pharmacology Biochemistry & Behavior*, vol. 49, no. 1

6   Berridge K et al., 2009, 'Dissecting components of reward: 'liking', 'wanting', and learning', *Current Opinions in Pharmacology*, vol. 9, no. 1

Interlude: A Mannish Jape

1   Comment on Murphy, J, 22 January 2014, 'How I lost weight by pledging to give money to a political party I loathe', *The Guardian*, https://www.theguardian.com/commentisfree/2014/jan/22/how-i-lost-weight-by-pledging-to-give-money-to-a-political-party-i-loathe

Chapter 6: Less Than a Loaf of Bread

1   Murphy, J, 20 July 2011, 'The old world order is toast', *Australian Financial Review*, p. 3

2   Hayek, F, 1945, 'The use of knowledge in society', *The American Economic Review*, vol. 35, no. 4

3   Smith, A, 1776, *An Inquiry into the Nature and Causes of the Wealth of Nations*

4   Bradford Delong, J, 16 May 2012, *Delong's Grasping Reality*, https://www.bradford-delong.com/2012/05/judt-and-hayek-crooked-timber-1.html

5   Hayek, 'The use of knowledge in society'

6   Hayek, 'The use of knowledge in society'

7   Hayek, 'The use of knowledge in society'

8   Hayek, 'The use of knowledge in society'

9   Whitehead, A, 1911, *An Introduction to Mathematics*

10   Smith, *An Inquiry into the Nature and Causes of the Wealth of Nations*

11   Smith, *An Inquiry into the Nature and Causes of the Wealth of Nations*

Chapter 7: Crazy Bargains (and Crazy Luxury)

1   *Trading Economics*, 2019, 'Baltic exchange dry index', https://tradingeconomics.com/commodity/baltic

2   World Bank Data, 2017, 'Container port traffic', https://data.worldbank.org/indicator/is.shp.good.tu

3   Pearce, F, 22 November 2009, *Daily Mail Australia*, 'How 16 ships create as much pollution as all the cars in the world', https://www.dailymail.co.uk/sciencetech/article-1229857/How-16-ships-create-pollution-cars-world.html

4   *BBC News*, 5 August 2014, 'Why so many shipowners find Panama's flag convenient' https://www.bbc.com/news/world-latin-america-28558480

5   McCullough, D, 1977, *The Path Between the Seas: The Creation of the Panama Canal, 1870-1914*

6   LVMH, 2019, 'Investors', https://www.lvmh.com/investors/
7   *LA Times*, 21 July 1898, page 12.

Chapter 8: Only the Fittest Survive

1   Fisher, I, 16 October 1929, 'Selling orders crack stock mart', *Belvidere Daily Republican*, p. 1
2   *New York Times*, 16 November 1930, p. 169
3   National Archives and Records Administration, 2012 United States Census, *Family Search*, https://www.familysearch.org/search/1940census/
4   Butts, A, 'Study of Games', cited in Fatsis, S, 2001, *Word Freak*
5   *Poughkeepsie Journal*, 18 September 1955, p. 4
6   Fatsis, S, 2001, 'Man of Letters', *University of Pennsylvania Gazette*
7   *The Pocono Record*, 24 June 1953, p. 26
8   *Montana Independent Record*, July 1953
9   Craft, R, 16 June 1957, *NYT Magazine*
10 *Mashable*, 7 December 2011, 'Alec Baldwin's words with friends addiction gets him booted off plane', https://mashable.com/2011/12/06/alec-baldwin/
11 Magie, E, 1902, 'The Landlord's Game', *The Single Tax Review*, https://landlordsgame.info/articles/LLG_SingleTaxReview-1902.html

Interlude: Dog

1   Manning, S, 26 January 2011, 'When animal rescuers become animal hoarders', *NBC News*, http://www.nbcnews.com/id/38978396/ns/health-pet_health/t/when-animal-rescuers-become-animal-hoarders/#.XL3QEqYRWvgr
2   Kobayashi, S and Schultz, W, 2008, 'Influence of reward delays on responses of dopamine neurons', *Journal of Neuroscience*, vol. 28, no. 30

Chapter 9: Self-perpetuating Incentives

1   *Hartford Courant*, 23 April 1935, p. 11
2   Mikkelson, D, 3 June 1997, 'Bill Gates' $5,000 giveaway' *Snopes*, https://www.snopes.com/fact-check/bill-gates-5000-giveaway/
3   Microsoft Answers, 2016, 'Email from Microsoft. Payment for forwarding email?', https://answers.microsoft.com/en-us/ie/forum/ie_other-windows_other/email-from-microsoft-payment-for-forwarding-email/29ca78e1-b69b-438d-a8b9-4a207c773b28?page=5
4   *Wired Magazine*, 1 July 2004, 'Copy this article & win quick cash', https://www.wired.com/2004/07/hoax/
5   Nakamoto, S, 2008, *Bitcoin: A Peer to Peer Electronic Cash System*, https://bitcoin.org/bitcoin.pdf
6   Kharif, D, 1 August 2018, 'Bitcoin's use in commerce keeps falling even as volatility eases', *Bloomberg*, https://www.bloomberg.com/news/articles/2018-08-01/bitcoin-s-use-in-commerce-keeps-falling-even-as-volatility-eases

7   Byrne, T, 24 February 2018, 'Pizza for lightning: Bitcoin legend Laszlo eats again!', *Bitsonline*, https://bitsonline.com/pizza-lightning-bitcoins-laszlo-hanyecz/

Chapter 10: Corruption and Rot

1   Max Planck (paraphrased)

2   Ioannidis, J, 2005, 'Why most published research findings are false', *PLOS Medicine*, vol. 2, no. 8, https://journals.plos.org/plosmedicine/article?id=10.1371/journal.pmed.0020124

3   Horton, R, 2015, 'Offline: What is medicine's 5 sigma?' *The Lancet*, vol. 385, no. 9976, https://www.thelancet.com/journals/lancet/article/PIIS0140-6736(15)60696-1/fulltext

4   Lee, SM, 25 February 2018, 'Here's how Cornell scientist Brian Wansink turned shoddy data into viral studies about how we eat' *Buzzfeed*, https://www.buzzfeednews.com/article/stephaniemlee/brian-wansink-cornell-p-hacking

5   Wansink, B, 15 December 2016, 'The graduate student who never said no', https://web.archive.org/web/20170312041524/http:/www.brianwansink.com/phd-advice/the-grad-student-who-never-said-no

6   Siğirci, Ö and Wansink, B, 2015, 'Low prices and high regret: how pricing influences regret at all-you-can-eat buffets' (retracted article), *BMC Nutrition*, vol. 1, no. 36

7   Comment on 'The graduate student who never said no'

8   Van Der Zee, T, 2017, 'The Wansink Dossier: an overview', *The Sceptical Scientist*, http://www.timvanderzee.com/the-wansink-dossier-an-overview/

9   Siegel, B, 2017, 'New study casts more doubt on "Smarter Lunchrooms" data', *The Lunch Tray*, https://www.thelunchtray.com/new-study-casts-more-doubt-smarter-lunchrooms-data/

10 Van Der See, 'The Wansink Dossier'

11 Brown, N, 28 November 2017, '"(Hundreds of hours of) work vindicated:" Critic of food researcher reacts to new retraction', *Retraction Watch*, https://retractionwatch.com/2017/11/28/hundreds-hours-work-vindicated-critic-food-researcher-reacts-new-retraction/

12 Chronicle Data, Cornell University, https://data.chronicle.com/190415/Cornell-University/faculty-salaries/

13 Kirschenbaum, K, 27 March 2013, 'Chronicle Report: dermatology professor makes $4.3 m salary', *Columbia Spectator*, https://www.columbiaspectator.com/2009/02/23/chronicle-report-dermatology-prof-makes-43m-salary/

14 Bednall, T, 13 July 2018, 'PhD completion: an evidence-based guide for students, supervisors and universities', *The Conversation*, https://theconversation.com/phd-completion-an-evidence-based-guide-for-students-supervisors-and-universities-99650

15 Milojevic, S, 2017, 'Changing demographics of scientific careers: The rise of the temporary workforce', *Proceedings of the National Academy of Science*, https://www.ncbi.nlm.nih.gov/pubmed/30530691?dopt=Abstract

16 Else, H, 28 November 2018, 'Does science have a bullying problem?', *Nature*, vol. 536, https://www.nature.com/articles/d41586-018-07532-5

17 Dayton, L, 9 February 2018, 'Australia faces a "postdocalypse" as young scientists take their brains and talent overseas', *ABC News*, https://www.abc.net.au/news/science/2018-02-10/postdocalypse-young-australian-scientists-taking-brains-overseas/9412276

18 Bhattacharjee, Y, 18 July 2011, 'How bad luck and bad networking cost Douglas Prasher a Nobel Prize' *Discover Magazine*, http://discovermagazine.com/2011/apr/30-how-bad-luck-networking-cost-prasher-nobel

19 Allan, N, 15 November 2013, 'Who will tomorrow's historians consider today's greatest inventors', *The Atlantic*, https://www.theatlantic.com/magazine/archive/2013/11/the-inventors/309534/

20 Davis, R, October 2016, 'Speech at 12th International IACFS/ME Research and Clinical Conference', https://www.youtube.com/watch?v=wz5we-QZ2Q4&t=638s

21 Norrie, J, 24 April 2012, 'Harvard: journal subscription fees are prohibitive', *The Conversation*, https://theconversation.com/harvard-journal-subscription-fees-are-prohibitive-6659

22 RELX, 2018 Annual Report and Financial Statements, https://www.relx.com/~/media/Files/R/RELX-Group/documents/reports/annual-reports/2018-annual-report.pdf

23 Science Europe, 2019, 'About', *cOALition S*, https://www.coalition-s.org/about/

24 Planck, M. 1949, *Scientific Autobiography and Other Papers*

25 The Royal Society, 1667, 'A narrative concerning the success of pendulum-watches at sea for the longitudes, *Philosophical Transactions of the Royal Society*, vol. 1, no. 1 https://royalsocietypublishing.org/doi/pdf/10.1098/rstl.1665.0011

Chapter 11: Justice

1 Transparency International, 2017 'Global Corruption barometer', https://www.transparency.org/news/feature/global_corruption_barometer_citizens_voices_from_around_the_world

2 Brosnan, S and de Waal, FBM, 2003, 'Monkeys reject unequal pay', *Nature*, vol. 245, see https://www.youtube.com/watch?v=meiU6TxysCg

3 *New World Encyclopedia*, 2017, 'Billy the Kid', http://www.newworldencyclopedia.org/entry/Billy_the_Kid

4 *The Inter Ocean*, 8 August 1902, 'Western Convict Sought', p. 1

5 *Bio*, 2019, 'Jesse James: Death of a Wild West Outlaw', https://www.biography.com/news/jesse-james-death-story

6 Traub, S, 1988, 'Rewards, bounty hunting, and criminal justice in the West: 1865-1900', *Western Historical Quarterly*, vol. 19, no. 3

7 Traub, 'Rewards, bounty hunting, and criminal justice in the West: 1865-1900'

8 *The Leavenworth Weekly Times*, 13 October 1892, p. 2

9 Traub, 'Rewards, bounty hunting, and criminal justice in the West: 1865-1900'

10 Mota, F, 1984, *The Adventures of Lafitte and the Pirates of Barataria*

11 *St Louis Post Dispatch*, 4 April 1882, p. 2
12 *The New York Times*, 18 April 1882, 'Jesse James's murderers: the Ford brothers indicted, plead guilty, sentenced to be hanged, and pardoned all in one day', https://www.nytimes.com/1882/04/18/archives/jesse-jamess-murderers-the-ford-brothers-indicted-plead-guilty.html
13 Miller, C, 18 February 2010, 'Jailed 16 years for murder he didn't commit, Greg Taylor tastes freedom', *CBS News*, https://www.cbsnews.com/news/jailed-16-years-for-murder-he-didnt-commit-greg-taylor-tastes-freedom/
14 Cusick, M, 20 November 2012, 'Scandals call into question crime labs' oversight', *NPR*, https://www.npr.org/2012/11/20/165579898/forensic-crime-lab-scandals-may-be-due-to-oversight
15 *Reason Magazine*, 23 August 2010, 'North Carolina's corrupted crime lab', https://reason.com/2010/08/23/north-carolinas-corrupted-crim
16 Koppl, R and Sacks, M, 2012, 'The criminal justice system creates incentives for false convictions', *Criminal Justice Ethics*, vol. 32, no. 2
17 Michael Risinger, D, 2006–2007, 'Innocents convicted: an empirical justified factual wrongful conviction rate', *Journal of Criminal Law & Criminology*, vol. 97, p. 761
18 Kelly, JF and Wearne, PK, 1998, *Tainting evidence: behind the scandals at the FBI crime lab*
19 Dror, IE et al., 2006. 'Contextual information renders experts vulnerable to making erroneous identifications', *Forensic Science International*, vol. 156, no. 1, https://www.sciencedirect.com/science/article/pii/S0379073805005876
20 Kershaw, S, 5 June 2004, 'Spain and US at odds on mistaken terror arrest', *The New York Times*, https://www.nytimes.com/2004/06/05/us/spain-and-us-at-odds-on-mistaken-terror-arrest.html
21 Kelly and Wearne, *Tainting Evidence*
22 National Research Council, 2009, *Strengthening Forensic Science in the United States: A Path Forward*, The National Academies Press
23 Vincent, F, 2010, 'Inquiry into the circumstances that led to the conviction of Mr Farah Abdulkadir Jama', Victorian Government

Chapter 12: Injustice, Armour and Fire

1 Kelly, N, 1879, 'The Jerilderie Letter', National Museum Australia, https://www.nma.gov.au/explore/features/ned-kelly-jerilderie-letter
2 Kelly, 'The Jerilderie Letter'
3 Report from the Select Committee on Police, 1852, https://www.parliament.vic.gov.au/vufind/Record/80033
4 Office of Police Integrity, 2007, 'Past Patterns, Future Directions: Victoria Police and the problem of corruption and serious misconduct', Victorian Government
5 Office of Police Integrity, 'Past Patterns, Future Directions'
6 1883 Royal Commission on Police, 'Special report on the Detective Branch', Victorian Government, https://digitised-collections.unimelb.edu.au/bitstream/handle/11343/21366/268756_UDS2010417-9.pdf

7   Dawson, S, 2015, 'Redeeming Fitzpatrick: Ned Kelly and the Fitzpatrick incident', *Eras Journal*, vol. 17, no. 1

8   Madden, E, cited in Eburn, M, 2005, 'Outlawry in Colonial Australia: The Felons Apprehension Acts 1865–1899', *ANZLH E-Journal*

9   *The Argus*, 14 February 1879, cited in Wright, B, 2011, 'In pursuit of the Kelly Reward: an examination of applicants to join the hunt for the Kelly gang in 1879', *Provenance: The Journal of Public Record Office Victoria*, vol. 10

10   *The Age*, 28 July 1879, p. 2

11   *The Age*, 1 July 1880, p. 3

12   *Town and Country Journal,* 10 July 1880, https://trove.nla.gov.au/newspaper/article/70945462

13   1881 Police Commission Progress Report of the Royal Commission of Enquiry into the Circumstances of the Kelly Outbreak, etc, Victorian Government

14   *The Australasian Sketcher with Pen and Pencil*, Saturday 3 July 1880, p. 150

15   *The Record*, 1 December 2016, 'The cleric and the bushranger; Perth priest part of historical siege at Glenrowan', https://www.therecord.com.au/news/local/the-cleric-and-the-bushranger-perth-priest-part-of-historical-siege-at-glenrowan/

16   *The New York Times*, 22 August 1880, p. 5

17   1881 Kelly Reward Board Report, Victorian Government, https://www.parliament.vic.gov.au/papers/govpub/VPARL1880-81No85.pdf

18   *The Telegraph Brisbane*, 21 March 1882

19   *The Age*, 21 April 1881

20   Hong Kong Independent Commission Against Corruption, 2016, 'Brief history', https://www.icac.org.hk/en/about/history/index.html

21   Manion, M, 2004, *Corruption by Design: Building clean government in mainland China and Hong Kong*, Harvard University Press.

Interlude: *The Hunger Games*

1   Collins, S, 2008, *The Hunger Games*

Chapter 13: Climate Change

1   Brimblecombe, P, 1976, 'Attitudes and responses towards air pollution in medieval England', *Journal of the Air Pollution Control Association*, vol. 26, no. 10

2   Earth System Research Laboratory, 2019, 'Trends in atmospheric carbon dioxide', https://www.esrl.noaa.gov/gmd/ccgg/trends/

3   NASA Scientific Visualization Studio, 2019, 'Global temperature anomalies from 1880 to 2018', https://svs.gsfc.nasa.gov/4626

4   US National Oceanic and Atmospheric Administration, 2018 Arctic Report Card, https://arctic.noaa.gov/Report-Card/Report-Card-2018/ArtMID/7878/ArticleID/783/Surface-Air-Temperature

5   Glennon, R, 21 April 2017, 'The unfolding tragedy of climate change in Bangladesh', *Scientific American*, https://blogs.scientificamerican.com/guest-blog/the-unfolding-tragedy-of-climate-change-in-bangladesh/

6   Gynther, I et al., 2016, 'Confirmation of the extinction of the Bramble Cay melomys Melomys rubicola on Bramble Cay, Torres Strait: results and conclusions from a comprehensive survey in August–September 2014', unpublished report to the Department of Environment and Heritage Protection, Queensland Government

7   National Oceanic and Atmospheric Administration, 2019, 'Biggest snowstorms (one foot or more) at Central Park (1869 to present)', https://www.weather.gov/media/okx/Climate/CentralPark/BiggestSnowstorms.pdf

8   NASA, 22 July 2010, 'Antarctica traced from space', https://www.nasa.gov/topics/earth/features/antarctica-outline.html

9   National Snow and Ice Data Centre, 'Facts about glaciers', https://nsidc.org/cryosphere/glaciers/quickfacts.html

10   *Nature*, 13 June 2018, 'Mass balance of the Antarctic Ice Sheet from 1992 to 2017', https://www.nature.com/articles/s41586-018-0179-y

11   Rignot, E et al., 2019, 'Four decades of Antarctic Ice Sheet mass balance from 1979–2017', *PNAS*, https://www.pnas.org/content/116/4/1095

12   Government Offices of Sweden, 'Sweden's carbon tax', https://www.government.se/government-policy/taxes-and-tariffs/swedens-carbon-tax/

13   Statistics Sweden, 2018, 'Total emissions and removals of greenhouse gases by greenhouse gas and sector, year 1990–2017', http://www.statistikdatabasen.scb.se/pxweb/en/ssd/START__MI__MI0107/TotaltUtslappN/?rxid=92da835b-4688-476e-8f5f-3df657fb27e0

14   *The New York Times*, 17 July 1989, 'Key sections of the Paris Communique by the Group of Seven', https://www.nytimes.com/1989/07/17/world/key-sections-of-the-paris-communique-by-the-group-of-seven.html

15   United Nations Framework Convention on Climate Change, February 2011, 'Fact Sheet: The Kyoto Protocol', https://unfccc.int/files/press/backgrounders/application/pdf/fact_sheet_the_kyoto_protocol.pdf

16   Kollmus, A and Schneider, L, 24 August 2015, 'Perverse effects of carbon markets on HFC-23 and SF6 abatement projects in Russia', *Nature Climate Change*, https://www.nature.com/articles/nclimate2772

17   *Christian Science Monitor*, 20 April 2010, 'Carbon offsets: how a Vatican forest failed to reduce global warming', https://www.csmonitor.com/Environment/2010/0420/Carbon-offsets-How-a-Vatican-forest-failed-to-reduce-global-warming

18   *ABC News*, 11 February 2013, '9pc drop in emissions from power generators', https://www.abc.net.au/news/2013-02-11/carbon-tax-emissions-drop/4512782

19   Australian Government Department of Environment and Energy Quarterly Update of Australia's Greenhouse Gas Inventory, September 2018, http://www.environment.gov.au/system/files/resources/4391288e-fc2b-477d-9f0b-99a01363e534/files/nggi-quarterly-update-sept-2018.pdf

20 Holden, R and Dixon, R, 21 November 2018, 'The carbon tax that would leave households better off while addressing climate change', https://www.abc.net.au/news/2018-11-21/the-carbon-tax-that-would-leave-households-better-off/10517652

Chapter 14: Ostrom

1 The Nobel Prize, 'Elinor Ostrom', https://www.nobelprize.org/prizes/economic-sciences/2009/ostrom/biographical/
2 The Nobel Prize, 'Elinor Ostrom'
3 Ostrom, E, 1990, *Governing the Commons*
4 Ostrom, *Governing the Commons*
5 Ostrom, *Governing the Commons*
6 Ostrom, *Governing the Commons*
7 Ostrom, E, 8 December 2009, 'Nobel Prize Lecture', https://www.nobelprize.org/prizes/economic-sciences/2009/ostrom/lecture/